THE HAMLYN CHILDREN'S WORLD ATLAS

Previous page: Mont St Michel in Normandy, France
Opposite page: Planting rice in Thailand

Front cover:
(right) Hungarian oil refinery/ZEFA Picture Library
(centre) Masai woman, Kenya/Tony Stone Worldwide
(left) Oil seed rape, Bulgaria/ZEFA Picture Library

Back cover:
(right) Alkmaar cheese market/Tony Stone Worldwide
(left) Abu Dhabi mosque/ZEFA Picture Library

Published in 1991 by
Hamlyn Children's Books, part of Reed International Books,
Michelin House, 81 Fulham Road, London SW3 6RB
Revised and reprinted 1992

Copyright © 1991 Ilex Publishers Limited

Text by Malcolm Day and Kate Woodward
Designed by Richard Rowan
Edited by Nicola Barber and Nicholas Harris
Maps produced by Euromap Limited
Illustrated by Janos Marffy (Jillian Burgess Artists) and
Chris Rothero (Linden Artists)

An Ilex Book

Created and produced by Ilex Publishers Limited,
29–31 George Street, Oxford, OX1 2AJ

ISBN 0 600 56872 5

Printed in Singapore

The heading strips in this book illustrate a famous or representative scene from each region,
as follows:

Page 6 Mount Everest, Himalayas, China/Nepal; p12 Iceland; p14 Carew Castle, Wales; p16
Eiffel Tower, Paris, France; p18 Windmills, the Netherlands; p20 River Rhine, West
Germany; p22 Matterhorn, Switzerland; p24 Leaning Tower, Pisa, Italy; p26 Sagrada
Familia, Barcelona, Spain; p28 Acropolis, Athens, Greece; p30 Budapest, Hungary; p32 St
Basil's Cathedral, Moscow, USSR; p38 Toronto, Canada; p40 New York, USA; p44 Chichén
Itzá, Mexico; p46 Caribbean beach; p50 Machu Picchu, Peru; p52 Rio de Janeiro, Brazil; p54
Atacama Desert, Chile; p60 Blue Mosque, Istanbul, Turkey; p62 Oasis, Saudi Arabia; p64
Village scene, Iran; p66 Taj Mahal, India; p68 Terraced fields, Indonesia; p70 Guilin, China;
p72 Mount Fuji, Japan; p76 The Sphinx and a Pyramid, Egypt; p78 Kilimanjaro, Tanzania;
p80 Cape Town, South Africa; p84 The harbour, Sydney, Australia; p86 Rotorua, New
Zealand; p88 Easter Island, Pacific; p90 Antarctica.

THE
HAMLYN
CHILDREN'S
WORLD
ATLAS

HAMLYN

CONTENTS

HOW TO USE THIS ATLAS

In this atlas the world is divided up into six parts: the continents of North America, South America, Europe, Asia and Africa, and the region known as Oceania which includes Australasia and the islands of the Pacific. At the beginning of each section you will find a political map showing the countries which make up each continent or region, together with facts and figures telling you about the area, population and capital of each of these countries. On the following pages, physical maps illustrate the land's surface, showing mountains, forests, deserts, ice, savanna, steppe and cultivated land.

To find out what the colours, symbols and abbreviations on the maps in this book mean, check the key on this page. If you want to look up a place, either on a map or in the text of this atlas, use the indexes at the back of the book.

Look at the location map to find out the position of a country or region in the world.

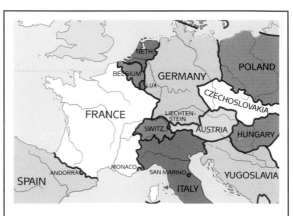

A political map shows how the world is divided into different countries.

KEY
Physical environments

Forest

Savanna/steppe/ cultivated land

Desert

Mountains

Tundra

Ice

Country border

State boundary

 Ottawa ■

Capital city

Milan ●

City (population over 1 million)

Puebla ●

City (population under 1 million)

Salem □

State capital

Olympus ▲ 2917

Mountain and height in metres

 Brenner Pass

Mountain pass

River

Seasonal river

Lake

Seasonal lake

Canal

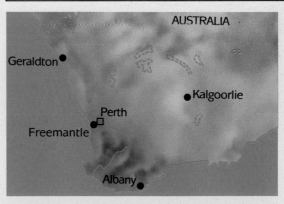

A physical map shows the mountains, lakes, deserts, forests and grasslands that cover the Earth's surface.

```
0                              200 Km
|-----|-----|-----|-----|-----|
0                              150 Miles
```

Abbreviations used on the maps in this atlas

Arch.	Archipelago
Aust.	Australia
Br.	(Great) Britain
C.	Cape
Fr.	France
I.	Island
Is.	Islands
L.	Lake
Mt.	Mount
Mts.	Mountains
Neth.	Netherlands
N.Z.	New Zealand
Pen.	Peninsula
Pk.	Peak
Port.	Portugal
Pt.	Point
Sp.	Spain
U.S.	United States of America

Abbreviations used in the text

km.	kilometres
sq. km.	square kilometres
m.	metres
cm.	centimetres
mi.	miles
sq. mi.	square miles
ft.	feet
in.	inches

Scale

The bar scale will enable you to work out real distances between two points shown on the map. Measure the number of centimetres on the map and then compare it to the number of kilometres or miles on the bar scale.

5

THE WORLD

This physical map of the world illustrates the surface of the Earth with its mountains, plains, deserts, lakes and rivers. Over two-thirds of the Earth's surface is covered by water. There are four vast oceans, the Pacific, Atlantic, Indian and Arctic. The seas surrounding Antarctica are sometimes counted as a fifth, known as the Southern Ocean. On this map the biggest ocean, the Pacific, is split into two.

Features in *relief* stand out on the map. You will see the Himalaya mountain range which contains the highest peaks in the world, and major river systems such as the Nile in Africa and the Amazon in South America. The gold-coloured areas represent the dry expanses of deserts, such as the Sahara, the Gobi Desert in central Asia, the arid lands of the Australian interior and the driest place on Earth, the Atacama Desert in Chile.

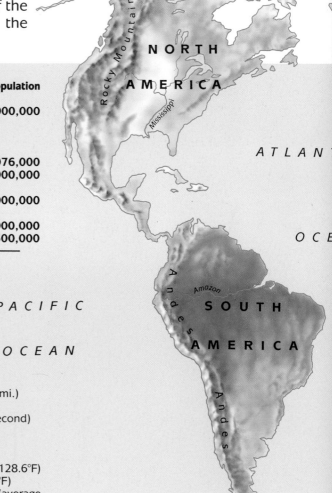

Regions of the World	Area		Estimated Population
	sq.km.	(sq.mi.)	
North America (including Mexico and Central America)	25,349,000	(9,785,000)	400,000,000
South America	17,611,000	(6,798,000)	271,076,000
Europe (including European Russia)	10,498,000	(4,053,300)	500,000,000
Asia (including Asian Russia)	45,066,000	(17,400,000)	3,000,000,000
Africa	30,335,000	(11,709,000)	555,000,000
Oceania	8,923,000	(3,444,278)	24,500,000
Antarctica	13,340,000	(5,149,240)	——

Earth Facts
Distance around the Equator 40,074km. (24,902mi.)
Distance around the Poles 40,008km. (24,860mi.)
Distance to the centre of the Earth 6370km. (3958mi.)
Average distance from the Earth to the Sun 150,000,000km. (93,210,000mi.)
Average distance from the Earth to the Moon 384,403km. (238,857mi.)
The Earth orbits the Sun at a speed of 29.8km. per second (18.5mi. per second)
Total surface area of the Earth 509,803,110sq.km. (196,836,000sq.mi.)
Total land area of the Earth 144,485,136sq.km (55,786,000sq.mi)
Total area of water on the Earth 365,318,000sq.km. (141,050,000sq.mi.)
Coldest recorded temperature on the Earth Vostok, Antarctica (−89.2°C/−128.6°F)
Hottest recorded temperature on the Earth San Luis, Mexico (57.8°C/136°F)
Place on the Earth with highest average rainfall Mount Waialeale, Hawaii (average annual rainfall 1168cm./460in.)
Driest place on the Earth Atacama Desert, Chile (no rain for over 400 years)

Largest Lakes	Area	
	sq.km.	sq.mi.
Caspian Sea (Asia)	371,000	(143,205)
Superior (Canada/USA)	83,270	(32,140)
Victoria (Africa)	69,484	(26,828)
Aral (Asia)	66,044	(25,500)
Huron (Canada/USA)	60,700	(23,430)
Michigan (USA)	58,020	(22,395)
Tanganyika (Africa)	32,900	(13,860)

Largest Deserts	Area	
	sq.km.	(sq.mi.)
Sahara	9,000,000	(3,475,000)
Australian	1,554,000	(600,000)
Arabian	1,295,000	(500,000)
Gobi	1,295,000	(500,000)
Kalahari	583,000	(225,000)

Highest Waterfalls	Drop	
	m.	(ft.)
Angel Falls (Venezuela)	979	(3212)
Tugela Falls (South Africa)	947	(3110)
Utigard Falls (Norway)	800	(2625)

Largest Islands	Area	
	sq.km.	(sq.mi.)
Australia	7,682,300	(2,966,151)
Greenland	2,175,601	(840,004)
New Guinea	800,510	(312,085)
Borneo	757,050	(292,000)
Madagascar	587,041	(226,658)
Sumatra	524,100	(202,300)
Baffin Island	476,065	(183,810)
Great Britain	229,870	(88,730)
Honshu	227,999	(88,031)

Longest Rivers	Length	
	km.	(mi.)
Nile (Africa)	6671	(4145)
Amazon (South America)	6615	(4050)
Mississippi-Missouri-Red Rock (North America)	6019	(3740)
Yangtze (China)	6300	(3915)
Ob-Irtysh (Russia, Kazakhstan)	5570	(3460)
Yenise (Russia)	5539	(3442)
Huang (Yellow River) (China)	5464	(3395)
Zaïre (Congo) (Africa)	4700	(2920)
Amur (Russia)	4416	(2744)
Lena (Russia)	4400	(2735)
Mackenzie-Peace (Canada)	4240	(2635)

Oceans	Area		Greatest depth
	sq.km.	(sq.mi.)	m. (ft.)
Pacific	165,240,000	(63,800,000)	11,033 (36,198)
Atlantic	82,439,355	(31,830,000)	9216 (30,238)
Indian	74,850,690	(28,900,000)	7725 (25,344)
Arctic	14,245,000	(5,500,000)	5500 (18,050)

Highest Mountains	Range	Height m. (ft.)
Mount Everest	Himalayas (China/Nepal)	8848 (29,028)
K2 (Godwin Austen)	Karakoram (China/India)	8611 (28,250)
Kanchenjunga	Himalayas (India/Nepal)	8586 (28,170)
Makalu 1	Himalayas (Nepal/China)	8463 (27,766)
Cho Oyu	Himalayas (Nepal/China)	8201 (26,906)
Dhaulagiri	Himalayas (Nepal)	8167 (26,795)
Manaslu	Himalayas (Nepal)	8163 (26,781)
Nanga Parbat	Himalayas (India)	8126 (26,660)

ARCTIC OCEAN

EUROPE

ASIA

Siberia

Gobi

Himalayas

AFRICA

Sahara

PACIFIC OCEAN

INDIAN OCEAN

AUSTRALIA

SOUTHERN OCEAN

EUROPE

This continent is made up of a number of small and densely populated countries. It extends from the Scandinavian countries in the north, which lie partly within the Arctic Circle, to the Mediterranean countries in the south. Also included is the European part of Russia, west of the Ural mountains. Europe contains the world's smallest country, Vatican City, which has fewer than 1000 inhabitants.

Climate and landscape differ enormously, from the cold uplands of Scandinavia and northern Russia, to the semi-desert conditions of parts of central Spain and southern Italy. A range of high mountains crosses southern Europe, forming the Pyrenees between France and Spain, the Alps (which run across Switzerland, France, Austria, Germany, Italy, and Yugoslavia), the Dolomites in Italy, and farther east the Tatra and Carpathian ranges. The highest mountain in

cont. page 10

BELGIUM
Official name Royaume de Belgique
Area 30,519 sq. km. (11,783 sq. miles)
Population 9,875,716
Capital Brussels (pop. 970,346)
Largest cities Antwerp (476,044), Gent (232,620) Charleroi (208,938) Liège (200,312) Bruges (117,857)
Currency Belgian Franc
Official language(s) Dutch (Flemish) and French (Walloon)
Chief products Cement, chemicals, glass, soap, cutlery, paper, steel, textiles, meat products (especially ham and pâté), cereals, dairy products, fish
Exports Iron and steel, textiles, copper, plastic products
Imports Machinery, vehicles, diamonds, oil, food

DENMARK
Official name Kongeriget Danmark
Area 43,092 sq. km. (16,638 sq. miles)
Population 5,129,254
Capital Copenhagen (pop. 1,351,999)
Largest cities Århus (195,152) Odense (137,286) Ålborg (113,650) Esbjerg (71,112) Randers (55,563) Horsens (46,735)
Currency Danish Krone
Official language(s) Danish
Chief products Bacon, poultry, eggs, cereals, livestock, fish, (especially cod, haddock, salmon), cement, diesel engines, electrical equipment, furniture, silverware
Exports Machinery, pork, other meat products, fish
Imports machinery, manufactured goods, iron and steel, textiles

FRANCE
Official name La République Française
Area 543,965 sq. km. (209,970 sq. miles)
Population 55,632,000
Capital Paris (pop. 2,188,918)
Largest cities Marseille (878,689) Lyon (418,476) Toulouse (354,289) Nice (338,486) Strasbourg (252,264)
Currency Franc
Official language(s) French (Breton and Basque are also spoken)
Chief products Aircraft, vehicles, aluminium, chemicals, electrical equipment, iron and steel, coal, jewellery, perfume, wine, cheese, cereals
Exports Machinery, vehicles, iron and steel, textiles, wheat, petroleum products, wine, cheese
Imports Machinery, oil, iron and steel, meat, textiles, fruit

THE NETHERLANDS
Official name Koninkrijk der Nederlanden
Area 41,160 sq. km. (15,891 sq. miles)
Population 14,757,848
Capital Amsterdam (pop. 691,738) (seat of government – The Hague)
Largest cities Rotterdam (574,299) The Hague (444,313) Utrecht (230,373) Eindhoven (191,002) Groningen (167,929),
Currency Guilder
Official language(s) Dutch
Chief products Natural gas, oil, salt, electrical equipment, clothing, iron and steel, machinery, vehicles, ships, dairy products, flowers, cereals
Exports machinery, textiles, chemical products, meat, flowers, vegetables
Imports Crude oil, vehicles, iron and steel, clothing

UNITED KINGDOM
Official name The United Kingdom of Great Britain and Northern Ireland
Area 244,103 sq. km. (94,249 sq. miles)
Population 56,617,900
Capital London (pop. 6,770,400)
Largest cities Birmingham (998,200) Glasgow (715,600) Leeds (709,000) Sheffield (532,300)
Currency Pound Sterling
Official language(s) English and Welsh
Chief products Oil, natural gas, coal, iron ore, steel, chalk, fish (especially cod, herring), chemicals, clothing, vehicles, cereals, machinery, dairy products
Exports Machinery, vehicles, textiles, electrical equipment, iron and steel, alcoholic drinks, aircraft
Imports Machinery, fruit and vegetables, diamonds, minerals, cereals, butter, meat, textiles

REPUBLIC OF IRELAND
Official name Poblacht Na L'Eireann
Area 68,895 sq. km. (26,595 sq. miles)
Population 3,538,000
Capital Dublin
Official language(s) Irish and English
Chief products Peat, potatoes, whiskey, beer, dairy products, linen, livestock, chemicals

ICELAND
Official name Island
Area 103,000 sq. km. (39,769 sq. miles)
Population 247,357
Capital Reykjavik
Official language(s) Icelandic
Chief products Fish and fish products, cement, aluminium, potatoes, turnips, fertilizers

NORWAY
Official name Kongeriket Norge
Area 323,878 sq. km. (125,050 sq. miles)
Population 4,198,289
Capital Oslo
Official language(s) Norwegian
Chief products Fish (especially cod and herring), timber, livestock, crude oil, natural gas

SWEDEN
Official name Konungariket Sverige
Area 440,945 sq. km. (170,250 sq. miles)
Population 8,458,880
Capital Stockholm
Official language(s) Swedish
Chief products Aircraft, vehicles, timber, minerals

FINLAND
Official name Suomen Tasavalta
Area 338,145 sq. km. (130,559 sq. miles)
Population 4,938,602
Capital Helsinki
Official language(s) Finnish and Swedish
Chief products Timber, paper, textiles, metals

The vineyards of Château du Pavillon in Bordeaux, France.

Europe
Highest point Mount Elbrus (Russia) 5633m. (18,481ft.) above sea level
Lowest point Shore of Caspian Sea (Asia) 28m. (92ft.) below sea level
Longest river Volga River (Russia) 3688km. (2290mi.)
Largest lake Lake Ladoga (Russia) 18,389 sq.km. (7100 sq.mi.)

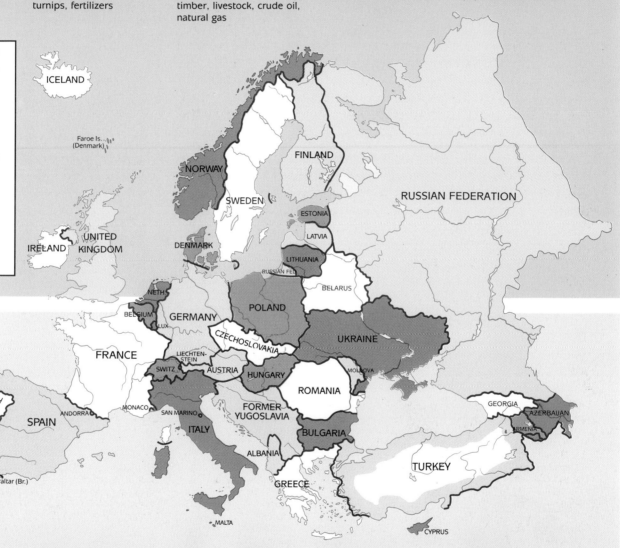

SPAIN
Official name España
Area 505,782 sq. km. (194,897 sq. miles)
Population 38,996,156
Capital Madrid (pop. 3,100,507)
Largest cities Barcelona (1,703,744)
Valencia (732,471)
Seville (655,435)
Zaragoza (575,317)
Málaga (566,330)
Currency Peseta
Official language(s) Spanish (Castilian) (Catalan, Basque and Galician are also spoken)
Chief products Vehicles, cement, iron ore, clothing, ships, steel, olives, wine, grapes, oranges
Exports Machinery, citrus fruits, vegetables, footwear, petroleum products, textiles, ships, olive oil, wine
Imports Crude oil, machinery, iron and steel, organic chemicals, maize, soya, wood, copper

ITALY
Official name Repubblica Italiana
Area 301,225 sq. km. (116,300 sq. miles)
Population 57,100,000
Capital Rome (pop. 2,821,420)
Largest cities Milan (1,511,193)
Naples (1,204,959)
Turin (1,034,007)
Genoa (733,990)
Currency Lira
Official language(s) Italian
Chief products Industrial and office equipment, domestic appliances, vehicles, textiles, clothing, chemicals, citrus fruits, wheat, maize, olives, wine
Exports Machinery, textiles, clothing, metals (especially mercury), chemicals, vehicles, footwear, leather goods
Imports Chemicals, metals and minerals, vehicles, agricultural products, food, machinery, oil

PORTUGAL
Official name República Portuguesa
Area 91,630 sq. km. (33,370 sq. miles)
Population 10,350,000
Capital Lisbon
Official language(s) Portuguese
Chief products Ships, textiles, citrus fruits, cork, leather goods, port, fish (especially sardines)

Floating logs downstream in Finland.

Europe is Mont Blanc which reaches 4813 metres, and which is situated on the border between France and Italy. Many famous rivers flow from these mountains. The Rhine has its source in the Swiss Alps and flows through Germany and the Netherlands. The Danube, which has its source in the Black Forest, flows east through seven countries before reaching the Black Sea.

Much of lowland Europe is intensively cultivated, being given over mostly to cereal crops or dairy herds. Local variations, however, give different regions very distinctive characters: olive groves and vineyards are widespread in countries bordering the Mediterranean or the Black Sea. Fruit orchards and the production of pigs and poultry are common throughout Europe, particularly in areas close to large conurbations, the major markets for local produce.

Haystacks in the Balkan Mountains in Bulgaria.

GERMANY
Official name Deutschland
Area 137,855 sq. miles
(357,042 sq. km.)
Population 77,812,298
Capital Berlin (pop.
3,300,636)
(administrative capital –
Bonn pop. 276,500)
Currency Deutsche Mark
Official language(s)
German
Chief products Minerals,
vehicles, steel, chemicals,
clothing, electrical goods,
livestock, beer, wine

RUSSIA
Area 17,076,811 sq. km.
(6,593,391 sq. miles)
Population 145,300,000
Capital Moscow
(pop. 8,967,000)
Currency Ruble
Official language(s)
Russian, plus 38 minority
languages
Chief products Coal, iron
ore, minerals, oil, gas, steel,
cereals, cotton
**See page 35 for
information on other
former Soviet republics.**

UKRAINE
Area 652,796 sq. km.
(252,046 sq. miles)
Population 51,200,000
Capital Kiev
Chief products Grain, coal,
iron and steel, sugar-beet,
machinery, chemicals

LITHUANIA
Area 26,173 sq. miles
(67,787 sq. km.)
Population 3,641,000
Capital Vilnius
Chief products Wheat,
lumber, potatoes, electrical
equipment

GEORGIA
Area 26,911 sq. miles
(69,700 sq.km.)
Population 5,449,000
Capital Tbilisi

ARMENIA
Area 11,506 sq. miles
(29,800 sq.km.)
Population 3,580,000
Capital Yerevan

ESTONIA
Area 17,413 sq. miles
(45,099 sq. km.)
Population 1,556,000
Capital Tallinn

MOLDOVA
Area 13,012 sq. miles
(33,700 sq.km.)
Population 4,341,000
Capital Kishniev

CZECHOSLOVAKIA
Area 127,905 sq. km.
(49,384 sq. miles)
Population 15,588,177
Capital Prague
Official language(s) Czech
and Slovak

POLAND
Area 312,683 sq. km.
(120,727 sq. miles)
Population 37,764,300
Capital Warsaw
Official language(s) Polish
Chief products Chemicals,
iron, steel, ships, coal

BELARUS
Area 207,976 sq. km.
(80,300 sq. miles)
Population 10,259,000
Capital Minsk

LATVIA
Area 24,695 sq. miles
(63,959 sq. km.)
Population 2,647,000
Capital Riga

AZERBAIJAN
Area 33,436 sq. miles
(88,800 sq.km.)
Population 7,145,600
Capital Baku

The EC building in Brussels.

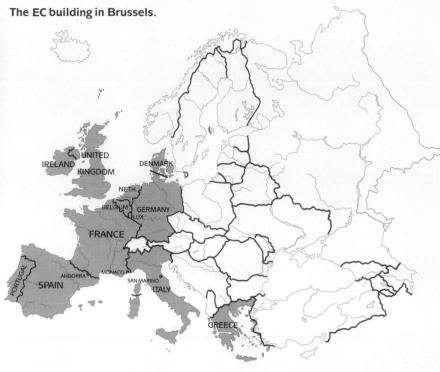

European Community

The European Community is an economic grouping of 12 of the Western European countries. It was formed to promote economic co-operation and co-ordination between its member states, in order to help them compete on equal terms with the economies of the USA and Japan. In 1951 the European Coal and Steel Community (ECSC) was established. This led, in 1957, to the creation of the European Economic Community (EEC) itself.

The European Parliament, formed in 1952, now has 518 members (MEPs), who are selected in local elections held in each country. The Parliament votes on economic policies relating to trade, agriculture and environmental issues.

Changes are to be introduced in 1992 which will create a single market within the European Community. Another major policy currently under development is monetary union, which aims to introduce a single currency for use in all of the member countries.

Member countries of the European Community:
Belgium
Denmark
France

Germany
Greece
Republic of Ireland
Italy
Luxembourg

The Netherlands
Portugal
Spain
United Kingdom

NAME	AREA SQ. KM. (SQ. MILES)	POPULATION	CAPITAL
Andorra	465 (180)	46,976	Andorra la Vella
Gibraltar (UK)	6.5 (2.125)	30,127	–
Liechtenstein	160 (62)	25,215	Vaduz
Malta	316 (122)	345,418	Valletta
Monaco	1.6 (0.65)	27,063	Monaco
San Marino	60.5 (23.4)	19,149	San Marino
The Vatican City	0.44 (0.17)	1000	–

 ANDORRA
 MALTA
 MONACO
 VATICAN CITY

*For the latest changes to Yugoslavia, refer to the map on page 29.

LUXEMBOURG
Area 2,585 sq. km. (998 sq. miles)
Population 367,200
Capital Luxembourg
Official language(s) French, Letzeburgish
Chief products Chemicals, iron, machinery, paints.

SWITZERLAND
Area 41,293 sq. km. (15,943 sq. miles)
Population 6,566,799
Capital Bern
Official language(s) German, French, Italian
Chief products Electrical equipment, chemicals

AUSTRIA
Area 83,855 sq. km. (32,377 sq. miles)
Population 7,576,000
Capital Vienna
Official language(s) German
Chief products Timber, chemicals, iron ore and steel

*FORMER YUGOSLAVIA
Area 225,804 sq. km. (98,766 sq. miles)
Population 23,411,000
Capital Belgrade
Official language(s) Serbo-Croar
Chief products Chemicals, metal products, copper

HUNGARY
Area 93,033 sq. km. (35,920 sq. miles)
Population 10,604,000
Capital Budapest
Official language(s) Hungarian
Chief products Coal, bauxite, wheat, sugar beet

ROMANIA
Area 237,500 sq. km. (91,699 sq. miles)
Population 22,940,430
Capital Bucharest
Official language(s) Romanian
Chief products Iron ore, oil, natural gas, machinery

BULGARIA
Area 110,912 sq. km. (42,823 sq. miles)
Population 8,973,596
Capital Sofia
Official language(s) Bulgarian
Chief products Cereals, electrical equipment, fruit

GREECE
Area 131,957 sq. km. (50,949 sq. miles)
Population 9,990,000
Capital Athens
Official language(s) Greek
Chief products Bauxite, lignite, cotton, tobacco, citrus fruits, olives, textiles

ALBANIA
Area 28,748 sq. km. (11,100 sq. miles)
Population 3,082,700
Capital Tiranë
Official language(s) Albanian
Chief products Textiles, petroleum products, wheat

CYPRUS
Area 9251 sq. km. (3572 sq. miles)
Population 673,000
Capital Nicosia
Official language(s) Greek and Turkish
Chief products Clothing, footwear, plastics, avocados

SCANDINAVIA AND FINLAND

The countries of Scandinavia (Norway, Sweden and Denmark), together with Finland and the island of Iceland lie in the north of Europe. These countries have small populations, and a high standard of living.

Norway, Sweden and Finland are all heavily forested, so lumbering – the felling of trees to make paper, furniture and other wood-based products – is an important industry. The warming influence of the Atlantic Gulf Stream brings with it huge shoals of cod, haddock, mackerel and herring; Norway, Denmark and Iceland all have large fishing industries. Norway has also benefited from the discovery, in 1970, of oil in the North Sea. Valuable supplies of iron ore and other minerals in Sweden supply its heavy industry which produces ships, Volvo and Saab cars, and aeroplanes.

Iceland's volcanoes and geysers attract many tourists during the short summer, and much of this volcanic power is harnessed to produce electricity.

Danish farming
Cheese-making in Denmark. Danish agriculture is centred on cattle, pigs and chickens and most of the crops grown in Denmark are used to feed this livestock.

Swedish logging mill
Trees are cut in the forests of Sweden and floated downstream to a logging mill where they are processed into pulp. This is then used to make paper.

A Norwegian fishing port
Sea fishing is one of Norway's most important industries. All the way up its long indented coastline there are fishing ports like this one, Hammerfest, in the far north of Norway.

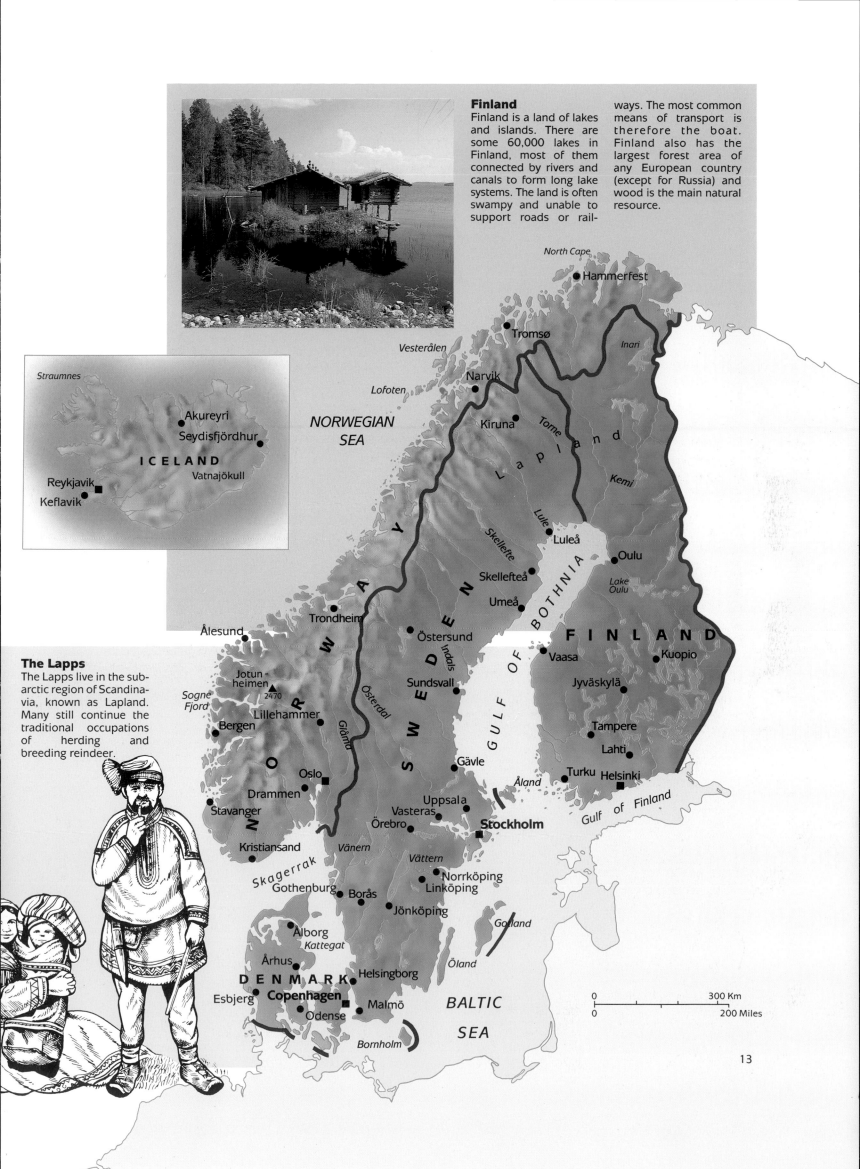

Finland

Finland is a land of lakes and islands. There are some 60,000 lakes in Finland, most of them connected by rivers and canals to form long lake systems. The land is often swampy and unable to support roads or railways. The most common means of transport is therefore the boat. Finland also has the largest forest area of any European country (except for Russia) and wood is the main natural resource.

The Lapps

The Lapps live in the sub-arctic region of Scandinavia, known as Lapland. Many still continue the traditional occupations of herding and breeding reindeer.

North Cape

Hammerfest

Tromsø

Vesterålen

Inari

Narvik

Lofoten

Straumnes

NORWEGIAN SEA

Kiruna

Torne

Lapland

Kemi

Akureyri

Seydisfjördhur

ICELAND

Vatnajökull

Reykjavik

Keflavik

Lule

Skellefte

Luleå

Oulu

Skellefteå

Lake Oulu

Umeå

GULF OF BOTHNIA

FINLAND

Trondheim

Östersund

Kuopio

Ålesund

Indals

Vaasa

Jotun-heimen

2470

Sundsvall

Jyväskylä

Sogne Fjord

Lillehammer

Österdal

SWEDEN

Bergen

Glåma

Tampere

Gävle

Lahti

Oslo

Turku

Helsinki

Drammen

Åland

Stavanger

NORWAY

Uppsala

Gulf of Finland

Vasteras

Örebro

Stockholm

Kristiansand

Vänern

Vättern

Skagerrak

Norrköping

Gothenburg

Borås

Linköping

Jönköping

Gotland

Ålborg

Kattegat

Öland

Århus

Helsingborg

DENMARK

Esbjerg

Copenhagen

Malmö

BALTIC

Odense

SEA

Bornholm

| 0 | | 300 Km |
| 0 | | 200 Miles |

13

BRITISH ISLES

The British Isles consist of the two main islands of Great Britain and Ireland, and a number of much smaller islands. The United Kingdom is made up of England, Wales, Scotland and Northern Ireland.

The position of the British Isles, near the warming influence of the Atlantic Gulf Stream, gives a mild climate. Cereal and vegetable crops grow well in the lowlands of southern England, while upland pastures in western and northern regions provide grazing for sheep and dairy cattle.

Britain's heavy industry grew up around the coalfields of central Scotland, northern England and south Wales. Ship-building, textile and steel-making industries were centred on cities such as Glasgow, Newcastle and Manchester, and Belfast in Northern Ireland. Now, half of Britain's exports come from the manufacture of electrical and engineering equipment, such as aircraft engines, cars, tractors and electronic devices. London, the capital of England, is a financial centre of international importance.

County Kerry, Ireland

The low green fields of central Ireland gradually rise to the high peaks on the south-western coast. The most westerly point in the British Isles is in County Kerry, where the full force of the Atlantic Ocean has made a rugged, indented coastline with high-sided river estuaries. Ireland's country-side has remained unspoilt partly because of a lack of industrial development.

The Lloyds Building, London

The new Lloyds Building, built in 1986, houses the world's most famous insurance company. The company originated in 1688 in Edward Lloyd's coffee house.

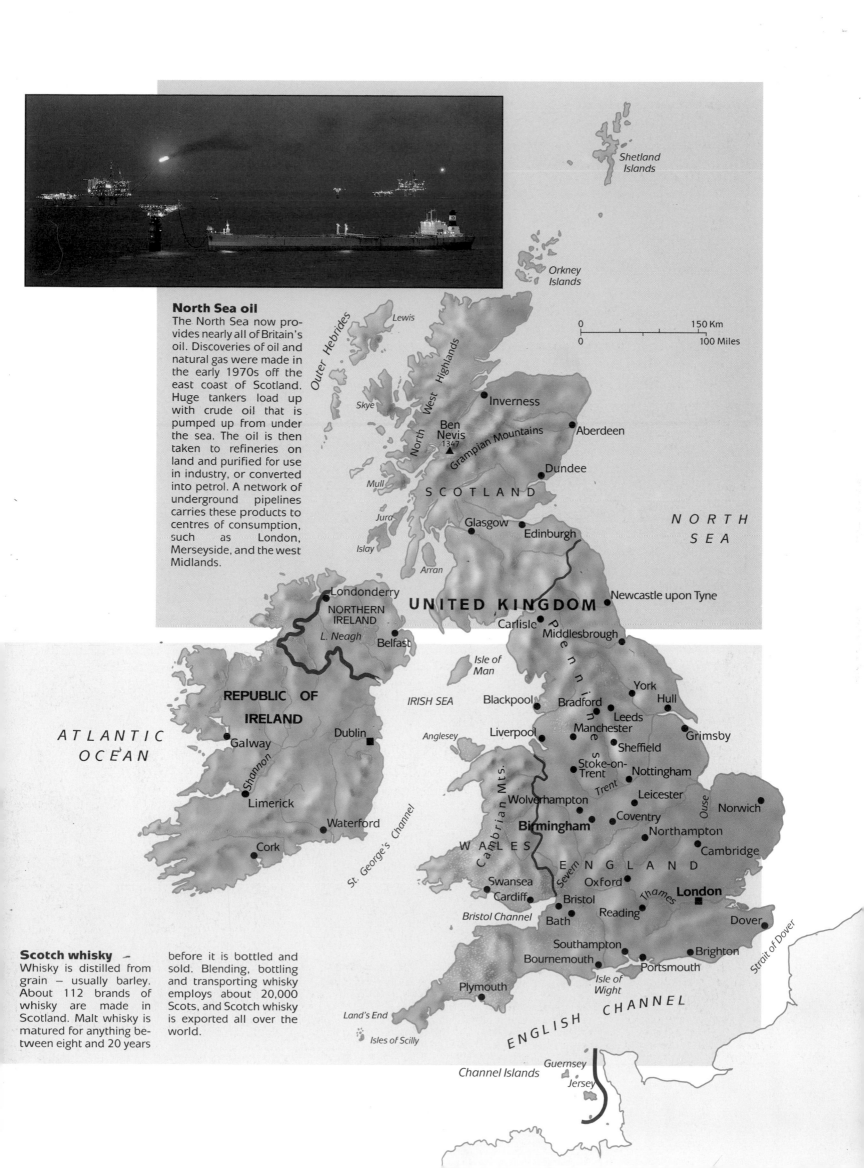

North Sea oil

The North Sea now provides nearly all of Britain's oil. Discoveries of oil and natural gas were made in the early 1970s off the east coast of Scotland. Huge tankers load up with crude oil that is pumped up from under the sea. The oil is then taken to refineries on land and purified for use in industry, or converted into petrol. A network of underground pipelines carries these products to centres of consumption, such as London, Merseyside, and the west Midlands.

Scotch whisky –

Whisky is distilled from grain – usually barley. About 112 brands of whisky are made in Scotland. Malt whisky is matured for anything between eight and 20 years before it is bottled and sold. Blending, bottling and transporting whisky employs about 20,000 Scots, and Scotch whisky is exported all over the world.

Shetland Islands

Orkney Islands

0   150 Km
0   100 Miles

Outer Hebrides

Lewis

Skye

NORTH WEST HIGHLANDS

Inverness

Ben Nevis 1347

Grampian Mountains

Aberdeen

Mull

Dundee

SCOTLAND

Jura

Islay

Glasgow

Edinburgh

NORTH SEA

Arran

Londonderry

NORTHERN IRELAND

L. Neagh

Belfast

UNITED KINGDOM

Newcastle upon Tyne

Carlisle

Middlesbrough

Pennines

Isle of Man

York

REPUBLIC OF IRELAND

ATLANTIC OCEAN

Galway

Dublin

IRISH SEA

Blackpool

Bradford

Hull

Leeds

Shannon

Anglesey

Liverpool

Manchester

Grimsby

Sheffield

Limerick

Stoke-on-Trent

Nottingham

Waterford

St. George's Channel

Cambrian Mts.

Wolverhampton

Trent

Leicester

Ouse

Norwich

Cork

Birmingham

Coventry

Northampton

WALES

Cambridge

ENGLAND

Severn

Swansea

Oxford

Thames

London

Cardiff

Bristol

Reading

Dover

Bristol Channel

Bath

Southampton

Brighton

Strait of Dover

Bournemouth

Portsmouth

Plymouth

Isle of Wight

Land's End

ENGLISH CHANNEL

Isles of Scilly

Channel Islands

Guernsey

Jersey

FRANCE

France is one of the richest nations in Europe, and is famous for its fine wines and good cooking. It is the largest country in Western Europe and ninety per cent of its land is suitable for farming. The mild temperatures and rain from the Atlantic Ocean, and farther south the warmer Mediterranean climate, provide suitable conditions for the cultivation of wheat, maize, artichokes, vines and tobacco.

The main industrial region lies in the north-east where there are important steel and engineering industries, including the manufacture of Renault and Citroën cars. But there are also newer centres for high-tech industry in the south, in areas around Toulouse, Marseille and Grenoble. Paris, the capital of France, has been a world centre of art and learning for hundreds of years. Today, it is also well-known for designer fashion, and for its perfume industry.

France is a country of widely differing landscapes. The French Alps are popular for skiing, while the Riviera along the Mediterranean coast is a fashionable beach resort.

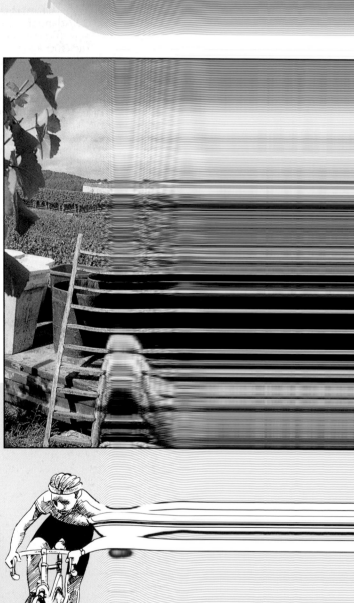

The Louvre
The Louvre in Paris was once one of the palaces of the kings of France. Today it is an art gallery, full of famous paintings, including Leonardo da Vinci's 'Mona Lisa', sculpture and antiquities. This glass pyramid is the latest addition to the Louvre buildings, forming a new entrance hall. It was commissioned by the French president, François Mitterrand.

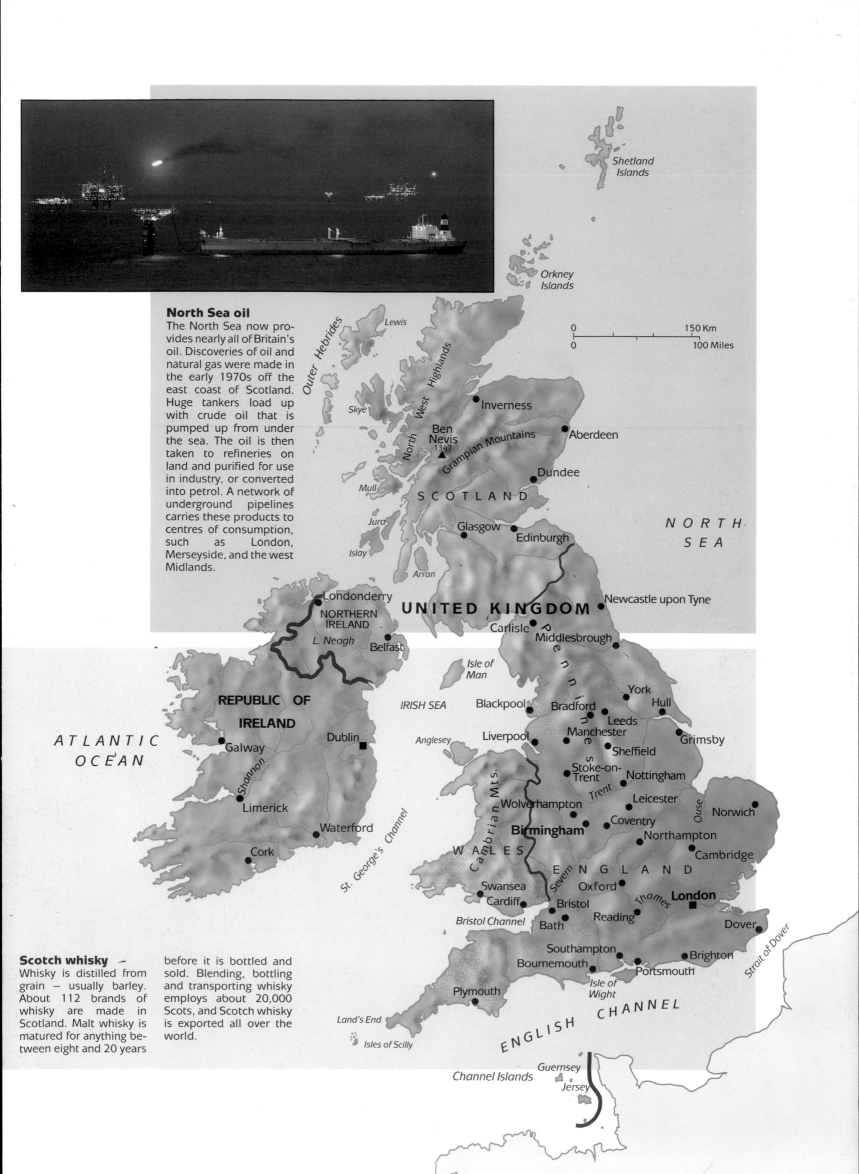

North Sea oil

The North Sea now provides nearly all of Britain's oil. Discoveries of oil and natural gas were made in the early 1970s off the east coast of Scotland. Huge tankers load up with crude oil that is pumped up from under the sea. The oil is then taken to refineries on land and purified for use in industry, or converted into petrol. A network of underground pipelines carries these products to centres of consumption, such as London, Merseyside, and the west Midlands.

Scotch whisky

Whisky is distilled from grain — usually barley. About 112 brands of whisky are made in Scotland. Malt whisky is matured for anything between eight and 20 years before it is bottled and sold. Blending, bottling and transporting whisky employs about 20,000 Scots, and Scotch whisky is exported all over the world.

Shetland Islands

Orkney Islands

Outer Hebrides

Lewis

Skye

North West Highlands

Inverness

Ben Nevis 1347 ▲

Grampian Mountains

Aberdeen

Mull

Dundee

SCOTLAND

Jura

Islay

Glasgow

Edinburgh

Arran

NORTH SEA

0   150 Km
0   100 Miles

Londonderry

NORTHERN IRELAND

L. Neagh

Belfast

UNITED KINGDOM

Newcastle upon Tyne

Carlisle

Middlesbrough

Pennines

Isle of Man

REPUBLIC OF IRELAND

IRISH SEA

Blackpool

York

Hull

ATLANTIC OCEAN

Galway

Dublin

Anglesey

Liverpool

Bradford

Leeds

Manchester

Sheffield

Grimsby

Shannon

Stoke-on-Trent

Nottingham

Limerick

Cambrian Mts.

Wolverhampton

Trent

Leicester

Ouse

Norwich

Waterford

Birmingham

Coventry

Northampton

Cork

WALES

ENGLAND

Cambridge

St. George's Channel

Swansea

Severn

Oxford

Thames

London

Cardiff

Bristol

Reading

Dover

Bristol Channel

Bath

Southampton

Brighton

Bournemouth

Portsmouth

Isle of Wight

Strait of Dover

Plymouth

ENGLISH CHANNEL

Land's End

Isles of Scilly

Channel Islands

Guernsey

Jersey

FRANCE

France is one of the richest nations in Europe, and is famous for its fine wines and good cooking. It is the largest country in Western Europe and ninety per cent of its land is suitable for farming. The mild temperatures and rain from the Atlantic Ocean, and farther south the warmer Mediterranean climate, provide suitable conditions for the cultivation of wheat, maize, artichokes, vines and tobacco.

The main industrial region lies in the north-east where there are important steel and engineering industries, including the manufacture of Renault and Citroën cars. But there are also newer centres for high-tech industry in the south, in areas around Toulouse, Marseille and Grenoble. Paris, the capital of France, has been a world centre of art and learning for hundreds of years. Today, it is also well-known for designer fashion, and for its perfume industry.

France is a country of widely differing landscapes. The French Alps are popular for skiing, while the Riviera along the Mediterranean coast is a fashionable beach resort.

The Louvre
The Louvre in Paris was once one of the palaces of the kings of France. Today it is an art gallery, full of famous paintings, including Leonardo da Vinci's 'Mona Lisa', sculpture and antiquities. This glass pyramid is the latest addition to the Louvre buildings, forming a new entrance hall. It was commissioned by the French president, François Mitterrand.

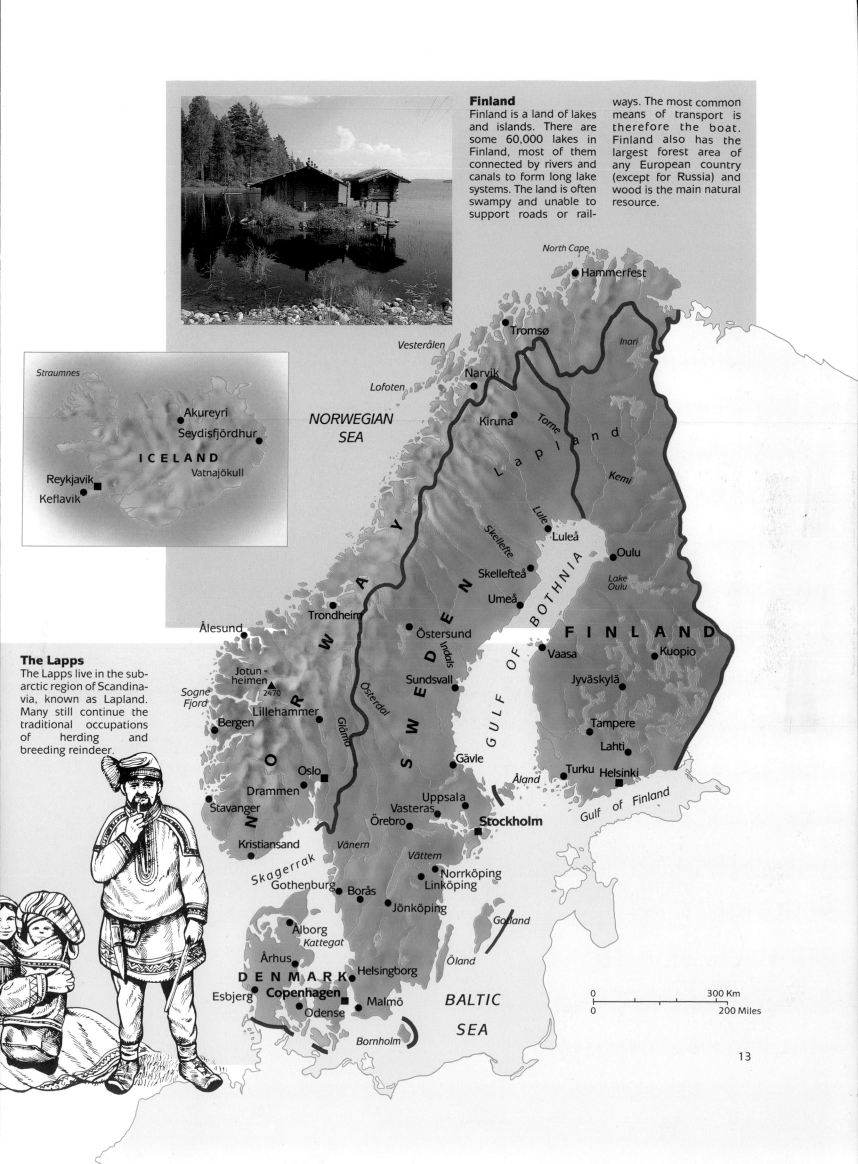

Finland

Finland is a land of lakes and islands. There are some 60,000 lakes in Finland, most of them connected by rivers and canals to form long lake systems. The land is often swampy and unable to support roads or railways. The most common means of transport is therefore the boat. Finland also has the largest forest area of any European country (except for Russia) and wood is the main natural resource.

The Lapps

The Lapps live in the sub-arctic region of Scandinavia, known as Lapland. Many still continue the traditional occupations of herding and breeding reindeer.

North Cape

Hammerfest

Tromsø

Vesterålen

Inari

Narvik

Lofoten

Kiruna

Torne

Lapland

NORWEGIAN
SEA

Kemi

Straumnes

Akureyri

Seydisfjördhur

ICELAND

Vatnajökull

Reykjavik

Keflavik

Lule

Luleå

Skellefte

Oulu

Skellefteå

Lake
Oulu

Umeå

GULF OF BOTHNIA

N
O
R
W
A
Y

Trondheim

Ålesund

Östersund

FINLAND

Jotun-
heimen
2470

Sundsvall

Indals

Vaasa

Kuopio

Sogne
Fjord

Lillehammer

Österdal

Jyväskylä

Bergen

S
W
E
D
E
N

Tampere

Glåma

Gävle

Lahti

Oslo

Åland

Turku

Helsinki

Drammen

Uppsala

Stavanger

Vasteras

Örebro

Gulf of Finland

Stockholm

Kristiansand

Vänern

Vättern

Skagerrak

Norrköping

Gothenburg

Borås

Linköping

Jönköping

Gotland

Ålborg

Kattegat

Öland

Århus

Helsingborg

DENMARK

Esbjerg

Copenhagen

Malmö

BALTIC

Odense

SEA

Bornholm

| 0 | 300 Km |
| 0 | 200 Miles |

13

BRITISH ISLES

The British Isles consist of the two main islands of Great Britain and Ireland, and a number of much smaller islands. The United Kingdom is made up of England, Wales, Scotland and Northern Ireland.

The position of the British Isles, near the warming influence of the Atlantic Gulf Stream, gives a mild climate. Cereal and vegetable crops grow well in the lowlands of southern England, while upland pastures in western and northern regions provide grazing for sheep and dairy cattle.

Britain's heavy industry grew up around the coalfields of central Scotland, northern England and south Wales. Ship-building, textile and steel-making industries were centred on cities such as Glasgow, Newcastle and Manchester, and Belfast in Northern Ireland. Now, half of Britain's exports come from the manufacture of electrical and engineering equipment, such as aircraft engines, cars, tractors and electronic devices. London, the capital of England, is a financial centre of international importance.

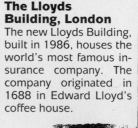

The Lloyds Building, London
The new Lloyds Building, built in 1986, houses the world's most famous insurance company. The company originated in 1688 in Edward Lloyd's coffee house.

County Kerry, Ireland
The low green fields of central Ireland gradually rise to the high peaks on the south-western coast. The most westerly point in the British Isles is in County Kerry, where the full force of the Atlantic Ocean has made a rugged, indented coastline with high-sided river estuaries. Ireland's country-side has remained unspoilt partly because of a lack of industrial development.

The TGV Atlantique

The TGV Atlantique is the first train in the world to travel at 300 kilometres per hour. New railway lines have been specially laid for the train which runs from Paris to the Atlantic coast in two hours. It is part of a modern network of high-speed railways which will eventually link up with Brussels, Amsterdam, Cologne, and London via the Channel Tunnel. The picture on the right shows the new TGV being constructed.

French wine

Vine cultivation is a cherished occupation in France. Each September the grapes are picked and taken to the presses. The grape juice slowly turns into high-quality wines such as Champagne, Burgundy and Bordeaux, which are named after the region they come from. French wines are exported all over the world.

The Tour de France

The Tour de France is the most popular sporting event in France. For three weeks in July, 150 cyclists race around France, climbing steep mountain roads and enduring high temperatures. A trail of TV camera crews, reporters, trainers and emergency services follows, and crowds line the route to offer their support.

Boulogne
Lille
Somme
Cherbourg
Le Havre
Amiens Picardy
Rouen
Oise
Caen
Reims
Meuse
Normandy
Paris
Marne
Metz
Brest
Champagne Nancy
Brittany
Seine Vosges
Quimper
Troyes Strasbourg
Rennes
Le Mans
Orléans
Plateau de Langres
Mulhouse
St.Nazaire
Angers Loire
Auxerre
Yonne
Doubs
Nantes
Tours
Cher
Dijon
Besançon
Bourges
Poitiers Vienne
F R A N C E
Burgundy
Saône Jura Mts.
La Rochelle
Roanne
Mt. Blanc 4810
BAY
Limoges
OF
Clermont-Ferrand
Lyon
BISCAY
Angoulême
Puy de Sancy 1885
Allier
St.-Étienne Grenoble
Périgueux
Dordogne
Massif
Bordeaux
Central Valence
Lot
Garonne
Rhône
Durance
Gascony
Nîmes Avignon
Nice
Bayonne
Toulouse
Montpellier
Cannes MONACO
Pau
Béziers
Marseille
Riviera
Toulon
Pyrenees
Perpignan
MEDITERRANEAN
SEA
Bastia

0   200 Km
0   150 Miles

Corsica
Ajaccio

BENELUX

Benelux is a name given to a group of three countries. BElgium, the NEtherlands (often known as Holland) and LUXembourg. The landscape of Holland and parts of Belgium is very flat, crisscrossed by canals and waterways. About 7700 square kilometres of land in Holland have been reclaimed from the sea by draining away the water and building dykes and barrages to keep the sea water out. Almost all the land is used for agriculture, specializing in dairy farming and horticulture.

All the Benelux countries are densely populated. In Belgium the country is split between Dutch- and Flemish-speaking Flemings in the north and French-speaking Walloons in the south. A large proportion of these people work in industry. Despite the fact that most raw materials have to be imported both Belgium and Luxembourg have heavy and light industries producing metals, textiles and chemicals as well as more specialized products such as soap and cutlery.

Esch-sur-Sûre
The Sûre River cuts its path through the wooded hills around Esch-sur-Sûre in northern Luxembourg. This region of Luxembourg and the Ardennes region in south-east Belgium are well-known for their beautiful natural scenery. Groves of walnut trees hide slate-roofed villages and remote castles. The Ardennes region is also renowned for its ham and pâté.

Rotterdam

Rotterdam is the world's busiest port. It is situated at the mouth of the Rivers Rhine and Maas which serve the industrial heartlands of Europe. Goods from the industrial Ruhr region of West Germany, for example, are taken downstream by barge to Rotterdam where they are lifted by crane on to ocean-going vessels. Huge oil tankers arrive from the Middle East bringing crude oil for the oil refineries and the many related petro-chemical plants that are located here. The Dutch oil company, Shell, can now send oil by pipeline direct from its refinery at the harbour to Amsterdam, Antwerp and West Germany. However, it is shipbuilding that is the most important industry in Rotterdam. Ever since the seventeenth century when the Dutch started trading overseas with the Far East, skilled craftworkers have been building merchant vessels. Today, their expertise is sought throughout the world by countries who need large container ships and supertankers.

Alkmaar cheese market

Alkmaar, a town near Amsterdam, is famous for its cheese market. Every Friday from April to October cheeses are put on display by cheese-porters who still wear a traditional costume dating from the sixteenth century. Alkmaar is a centre for the dairy industry which is the main form of agriculture in the Netherlands. The warm waters of the Gulf Stream bring mild winters and wet summers which help to produce a long growing season and excellent grazing land for cattle.

The Atomium

The Atomium is an aluminium structure that was built for the World Fair in 1958 in Brussels. It is intended to represent a molecule of an iron crystal, magnified 265 million times. Each sphere is an atom, making up a total of nine atoms in the molecule. The three lower atoms now house an exhibition on the peaceful use of nuclear energy. You can take escalators up the tubes to reach a restaurant in the top sphere.

GERMANY

After World War II Germany was divided into two – the Federal Republic of Germany (West Germany), and the German Democratic Republic (East Germany), which traded almost exclusively with other Eastern European countries. In 1989, restrictions on freedom of travel and communication between them were lifted for the first time since the war, and the two countries were unified as one, united Germany in October 1990.

Germany is a leading industrial nation. It has large natural reserves of coal and iron ore, and the Ruhr valley is one of the most important industrial centres in Europe. The Rhine is a vital route for industrial cargo, handled by ports such as Mannheim, Cologne and Duisburg. Germany also has traditional centres of manufacturing such as Dresden, famous for its china.

The northern region of Germany is a lowland plain – farther south the land is more mountainous and heavily forested. The coniferous forests and remote castles of the Black Forest and Bavarian Alps attract many tourists.

Coal-cutting in the Ruhr
Lignite, also known as brown coal, is being excavated at this open-cast mine in the Ruhr district. Modern equipment can dig out the coal quickly and efficiently. The Ruhr is one of the largest industrial areas in Europe.

Rothenburg on the Tauber
Rothenburg on the Tauber is in Bavaria in the south of Germany. It is one of the best preserved medieval towns in Germany, and little has changed in 400 years. All its walls, towers, high-gabled houses and narrow crooked streets date from that time. Traditional crafts such as woodcarving are still practised.

German industry

Germany is one of the biggest industrial nations in the world. It is well-known for its manufacturing industries, electrical equipment, machinery, chemicals and cars such as BMW and Volkswagen. It has a highly-skilled workforce (the woman in the picture is working on a Praktica camera). However, despite the natural resources of areas such as the Ruhr valley, most fuel and other raw materials are in short supply and must be imported.

The Brandenburg Gate

The Brandenburg Gate stands to the east side of the now dismantled Wall in Berlin. It has changed from being a symbol of German division to one of German unity. The Wall in Berlin was put up after World War II to partition the city of Berlin.

East Berlin became the capital of East Germany, but West Berlin became an isolated pocket of West Germany inside the East German frontier. Until 1989 no-one, from the East or West, could cross the Wall except under special circumstances. Now the Wall has been dismantled and families and friends who were separated for over 40 years are free to see each other again.

0   200 Km
0   150 Miles

NORTH SEA

BALTIC SEA

Rügen

Flensburg
Kiel
Lübeck
Stralsund
Rostock
Schwerin
Wilhelmshaven
Hamburg
Oldenburg
Bremen
Lower Saxony
Elbe
Ems
Weser
Osnabrück
Hannover
Braunschweig
Berlin
Potsdam
Magdeburg
Oder
Frankfurt
Bielefeld
Salzgitter
Münster
Harz Mts.
Cottbus
Dortmund
Duisburg
Essen
Ruhr
Kassel
Halle
Leipzig
Elbe
Düsseldorf
G E R M A N Y
Dresden
Cologne
Bonn
Rhine
Errurt
Zwickau
Karl Marx Stadt (Chemnitz)
Eifel
Thuringian Forest
Moselle
Wiesbaden
Frankfurt
Mainz
Würzburg
Main
Bohemian Forest
Mannheim
Saarbrücken
Neckar
Nürnberg
Karlsruhe
Stuttgart
Regensburg
Freiburg
Black Forest
Danube
Augsburg
Munich
Isar
Bavaria
L. Constance
A l p s

21

AUSTRIA AND SWITZERLAND

Austria and Switzerland are the most mountainous countries in Europe, with the Alps covering three-quarters of their land. Much of the people's way of life is dictated by this environment.

Since the sixteenth century Switzerland has had a policy of neutrality in times of war. This reputation for neutrality and security has made Switzerland one of the world's most important centres for banking.

Neither Austria nor Switzerland have reserves of oil or coal, and as a result water-power from the mountain rivers is a vital source of energy. Austria also relies heavily on Eastern European countries for its energy supplies. Swiss workers make high-quality products such as watches and scientific instruments while Austria has big chemical and manufacturing industries. Tourism is extremely important in both countries: there are many famous ski resorts, and Vienna, the capital of Austria, is one of the great cultural centres of the world.

Swiss commerce
Switzerland has long had a tradition of neutrality and security. As a result it has become an important centre for international commerce and banking. The Swiss city, Geneva, is also the European headquarters for international organizations such as the Red Cross and the United Nations, and has often been used by other countries to stage peace talks.

Ski-school at Verbier

Most Swiss children feel at home on skis by the age of seven. Local primary schools give lessons on the slopes, and there are special ski-schools to develop technique at an early age. Verbier is a big ski resort which attracts skiers from all over Europe every winter.

The Tyrol

The far western arm of Austria is part of a region known as the Tyrol. It is one of the highest Alpine areas and also one of the most traditional. The province was founded in the fourteenth century and is still regarded by its inhabitants as distinct from the modern states of Austria and Italy across which it lies.

Prater Park

This fairground wheel in Prater Park in Vienna, the capital of Austria, is one of the largest in Europe.

Salzburg

Salzburg lies just inside the border between Austria and West Germany. It is the birthplace of the famous composer, Mozart. Every summer there is a music festival in celebration of Mozart's operas and chamber music. Thousands of people come from all over Europe to enjoy the festival, and all the restaurants and hotels are full.

23

ITALY

Italy juts into the Mediterranean Sea and includes the two islands of Sicily, at its foot, and Sardinia to the west. It is one of the youngest countries in Europe — its various kingdoms were not united until 1870.

Italy ranks among the richer nations of the world, yet there is a huge difference between the standard of living in the prosperous, industrial north and the poorer, mainly agricultural south. Rome may be the capital of Italy, but Milan in the north is its business, financial and industrial capital and an international centre for fashion and design. In addition trades such as glass-blowing, shoe-making and weaving textiles for high-quality clothes are still practised in various traditional centres. However, Italy has limited natural resources and imports both oil and electricity.

In the south, olives and citrus fruits are grown, but the most fertile agricultural area is the Po valley in the north. Vines are grown on the slopes of the Apennine mountains.

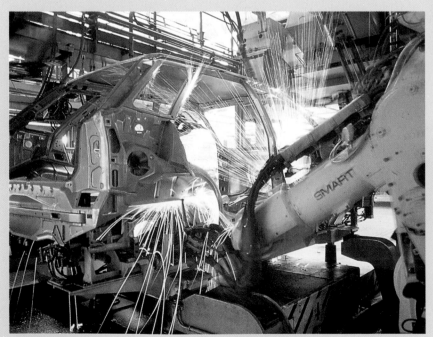

Vatican City
The Vatican is a separate city within Rome, from where the Pope leads the Roman Catholic Church world-wide. As well as being the smallest country in the world, with an area of less than one square kilometre, it is also the only place where Latin is the official language. It has its own bank, telephone and postal system as well as a small army called the Swiss Guard to protect the Pope himself.

Italy's industry
Italy's biggest manufacturing company is Fiat Motor Cars based in Turin. This company has one of the most up-to-date methods of car production in the world. Robots are used for complete precision in every process — assembling, welding and painting.

24

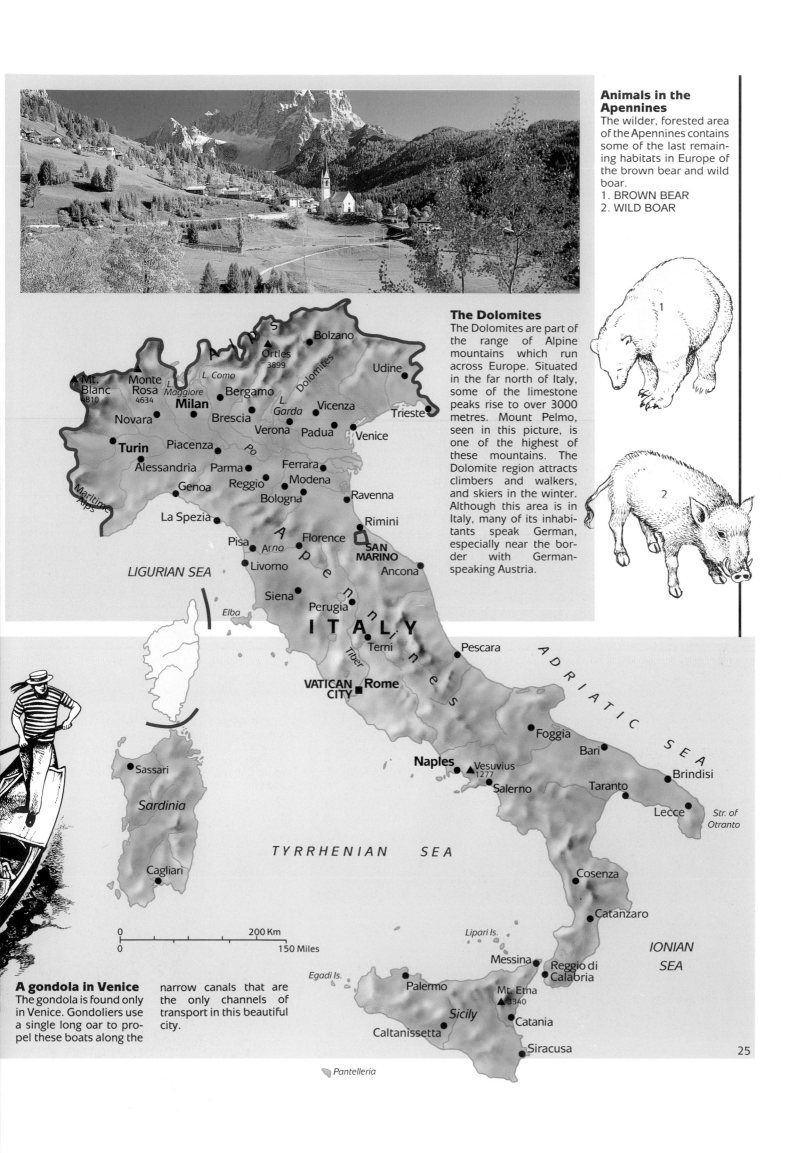

Animals in the Apennines

The wilder, forested area of the Apennines contains some of the last remaining habitats in Europe of the brown bear and wild boar.
1. BROWN BEAR
2. WILD BOAR

The Dolomites

The Dolomites are part of the range of Alpine mountains which run across Europe. Situated in the far north of Italy, some of the limestone peaks rise to over 3000 metres. Mount Pelmo, seen in this picture, is one of the highest of these mountains. The Dolomite region attracts climbers and walkers, and skiers in the winter. Although this area is in Italy, many of its inhabitants speak German, especially near the border with German-speaking Austria.

A gondola in Venice

The gondola is found only in Venice. Gondoliers use a single long oar to propel these boats along the narrow canals that are the only channels of transport in this beautiful city.

ALPS

Bolzano
Ortles 3899
Udine
Mt. Blanc 4810
Monte Rosa 4634
L. Maggiore
L. Como
Dolomites
Bergamo
Milan
L. Garda
Vicenza
Trieste
Novara
Brescia
Verona
Padua
Venice
Turin
Piacenza
Po
Alessandria
Parma
Ferrara
Genoa
Reggio
Modena
Maritime Alps
Bologna
Ravenna
La Spezia
Rimini
Pisa
Arno
Florence
SAN MARINO
Livorno
Ancona
LIGURIAN SEA
Siena
Elba
Perugia
ITALY
Terni
Pescara
Tiber
VATICAN CITY
Rome
ADRIATIC SEA
Foggia
Bari
Naples
Vesuvius 1277
Brindisi
Sassari
Salerno
Taranto
Lecce
Str. of Otranto
Sardinia
Cosenza
Cagliari
TYRRHENIAN SEA
Catanzaro
0   200 Km
0   150 Miles
Lipari Is.
IONIAN SEA
Messina
Reggio di Calabria
Egadi Is.
Palermo
Mt. Etna 3340
Catania
Sicily
Caltanissetta
Siracusa
Pantelleria

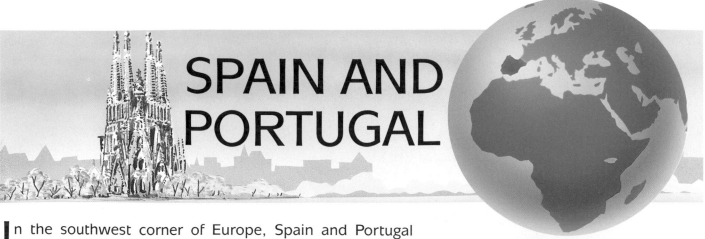

SPAIN AND PORTUGAL

In the southwest corner of Europe, Spain and Portugal form the Iberian Peninsula. Spain is the second largest country in western Europe but it has only the fifth largest population. Spanish is one of four languages spoken – and almost a quarter of the Spanish speakers use dialects other than the offical Castilian Spanish.

Since 1930 much of the Spanish population has moved away from the countryside to live and work in the main cities and industrial centres. The chemical industry, shipbuilding, steel production and tourism are all important for Spain's economy. Spain also exports agricultural products, including olive oil, citrus fruit and sherry from the Jerez region.

Portugal was less developed than Spain, but industry is now becoming more important. Tourism and the export of textiles are the traditional mainstays; in addition most of Europe's supply of cork comes from special oak trees in the south of the country.

Olive groves in Andalusia
Olives, which need little water, grow well in Andalusia in the south of Spain, where it is hot and dry. Most are crushed to make olive oil.

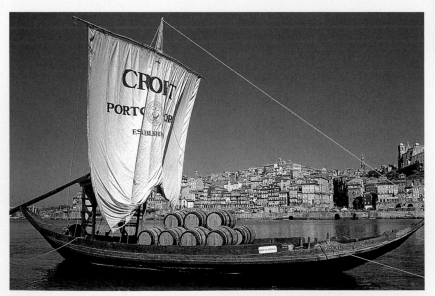

Oporto port
Portugal is famous for its port, a dark red wine usually drunk after dinner. It is made at vineyards along the Douro River, then put into casks and taken downstream by barge to Oporto, the city named after the wine. Here, the port is stored in cellars, called 'Lodges', and may be left to mature for ten to twenty years before being shipped all over the world.

Bull-fighting
Every Sunday evening in Spain during the summer, crowds assemble in bullrings around the country. They watch and cheer as their favourite matador flicks his scarlet cape at the charging bull.

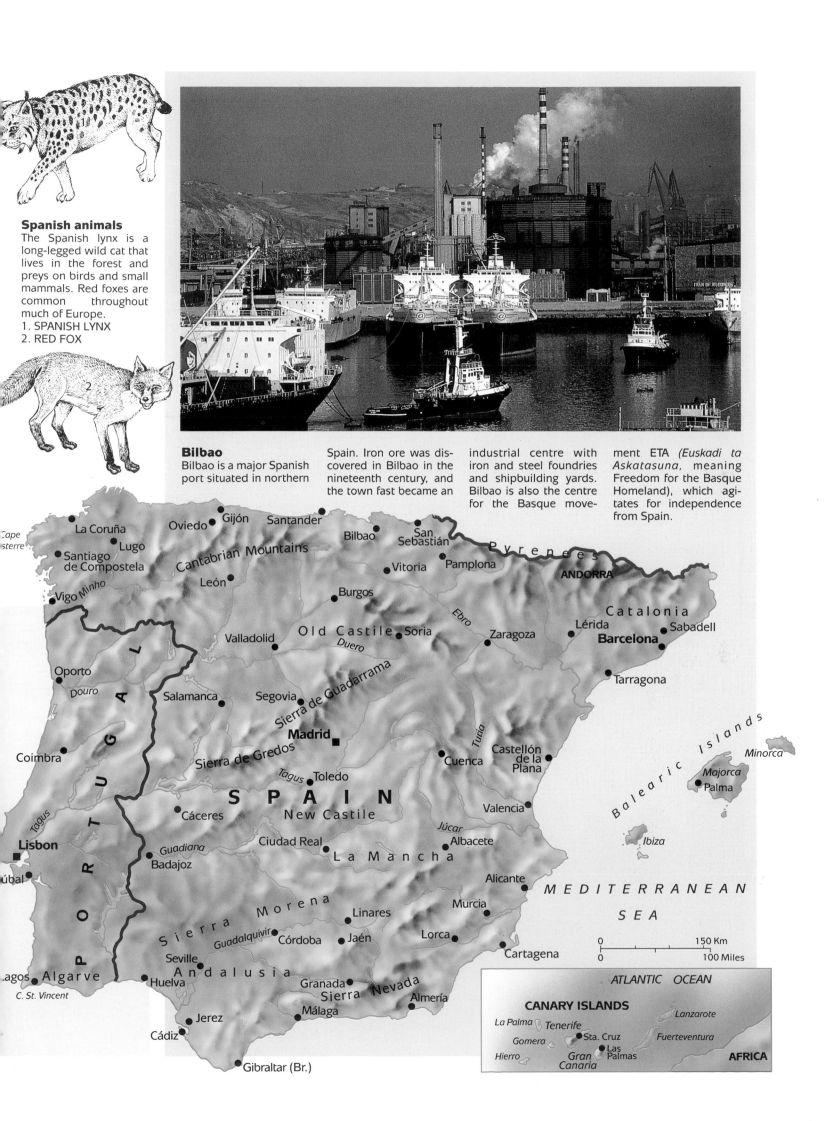

Spanish animals

The Spanish lynx is a long-legged wild cat that lives in the forest and preys on birds and small mammals. Red foxes are common throughout much of Europe.
1. SPANISH LYNX
2. RED FOX

Bilbao

Bilbao is a major Spanish port situated in northern Spain. Iron ore was discovered in Bilbao in the nineteenth century, and the town fast became an industrial centre with iron and steel foundries and shipbuilding yards. Bilbao is also the centre for the Basque movement ETA *(Euskadi ta Askatasuna,* meaning Freedom for the Basque Homeland), which agitates for independence from Spain.

SOUTH-EAST EUROPE

Yugoslavia, Romania, Bulgaria, Greece and Albania are often known as the Balkan countries. They lie at the extreme south-east of Europe, close to Asia. In the past many different European and Asian peoples have settled in this area, resulting in the present mixture of people, languages and religions.

Much of the region is mountainous. The river Danube, which forms the boundary between Romania and Bulgaria before flowing into the Black Sea, is surrounded by fertile, heavily-cultivated land. Much of the produce is sold in local markets but Bulgaria exports agricultural goods such as canned fruits and vegetables and Greece exports olive oil and citrus fruits.

Heavy industry plays an important part in the economies of these countries; Bulgaria also has a fast-growing electronics industry. Yugoslavia is the leading European producer of copper, while Greece is a shipping centre. Tourism is also extremely important, especially for Greece.

A fruit market in Dubrovnik
Dubrovnik is an old walled sea-port on the Adriatic coast of Yugoslavia. It is also a market centre for products such as cheese, milk, wood, olives and grapes brought from neighbouring villages.

Meteora, Greece
There are many monasteries in the beautiful mountainous countryside of Greece. The monasteries at Meteora in central Greece are set on top of a pinnacle of rock. To reach them, before steps were cut, people were hauled up the side in a basket.

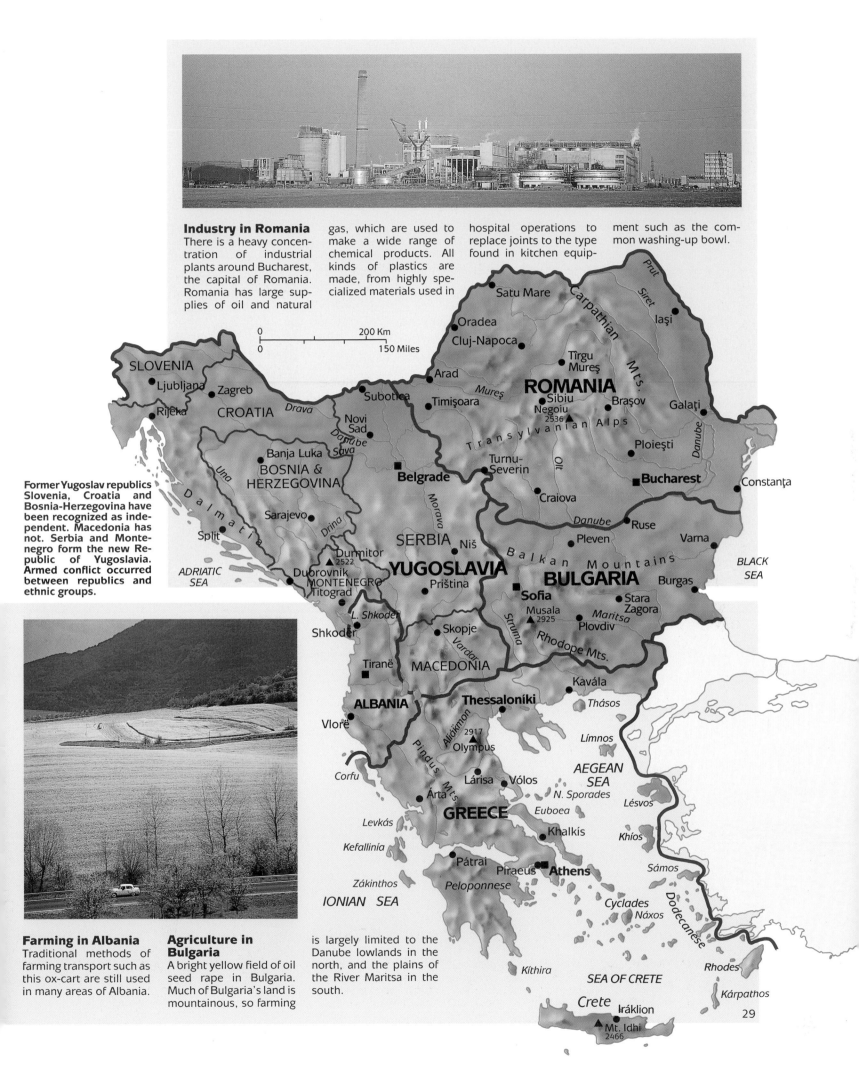

Industry in Romania

There is a heavy concentration of industrial plants around Bucharest, the capital of Romania. Romania has large supplies of oil and natural gas, which are used to make a wide range of chemical products. All kinds of plastics are made, from highly specialized materials used in hospital operations to replace joints to the type found in kitchen equipment such as the common washing-up bowl.

Former Yugoslav republics Slovenia, Croatia and Bosnia-Herzegovina have been recognized as independent. Macedonia has not. Serbia and Montenegro form the new Republic of Yugoslavia. Armed conflict occurred between republics and ethnic groups.

Farming in Albania

Traditional methods of farming transport such as this ox-cart are still used in many areas of Albania.

Agriculture in Bulgaria

A bright yellow field of oil seed rape in Bulgaria. Much of Bulgaria's land is mountainous, so farming is largely limited to the Danube lowlands in the north, and the plains of the River Maritsa in the south.

29

CENTRAL EUROPE

Czechoslovakia, Poland, and Hungary form part of central Europe. Poland and Hungary are both mainly lowland countries, and Hungary is heavily forested. Czechoslovakia is more mountainous. The climate throughout this region is temperate, but winters can be extremely cold, and ice often closes the harbors along the Polish Baltic coast.

Poland and Czechoslovakia are rich in natural resources and are both heavily industrialized. Poland mines coal, mainly from coalfields in Silesia, which is both exported and used to supply the steel and shipbuilding industries based around Gdansk on the Baltic coast. Large deposits of gold were found in Czechoslavakia in the mid-1980s, uranium is also mined in the mountains and used to produce nuclear power.

South of Budapest, the beautiful capital city of Hungary, the land surrounding the River Danube is particularly fertile and crops such as wheat, sugar beet and potatoes are grown.

Refining oil
This maze of pipes and tanks is necessary for the complex process of oil production. Czechoslovakia, Poland, and Hungary do not have large natural reserves of oil, so all three countries are forced to import crude oil from abroad. When crude oil is taken from below the ground or sea it has to be refined, so that it can be separated into oil, petrol, paraffin, and other products. This oil refinery is in Szazhalombatta, near Budapest, the capital of Hungary.

Polish traditional dress
In some rural areas Polish men and women still wear traditional dress. The strong, well-made garments last for a long time. These costumes are also worn for festivals and folk-dances which are an important part of popular culture all over Eastern Europe. Especially in the rural areas, traditional customs have been passed down from generation to generation and kept alive.

Charles Bridge, Prague
The city of Prague, capital of Czechoslovakia, was a major European cultural centre in medieval times. Much of the beautiful architecture remains, and now the old palaces house government institutions and academies of music and art.

Agriculture in Poland

Rolling green fields typical of Poland's central agricultural region. Most of the farmland is planted with crops to grow feed for pigs and chickens. Farming machinery is usually old-fashioned and frequently there are no fertilizers to help crops to grow in the poorer soils. Distribution of farm produce to the market centres can also be difficult. There are sometimes food shortages and people often have to queue for hours to buy meat or bread.

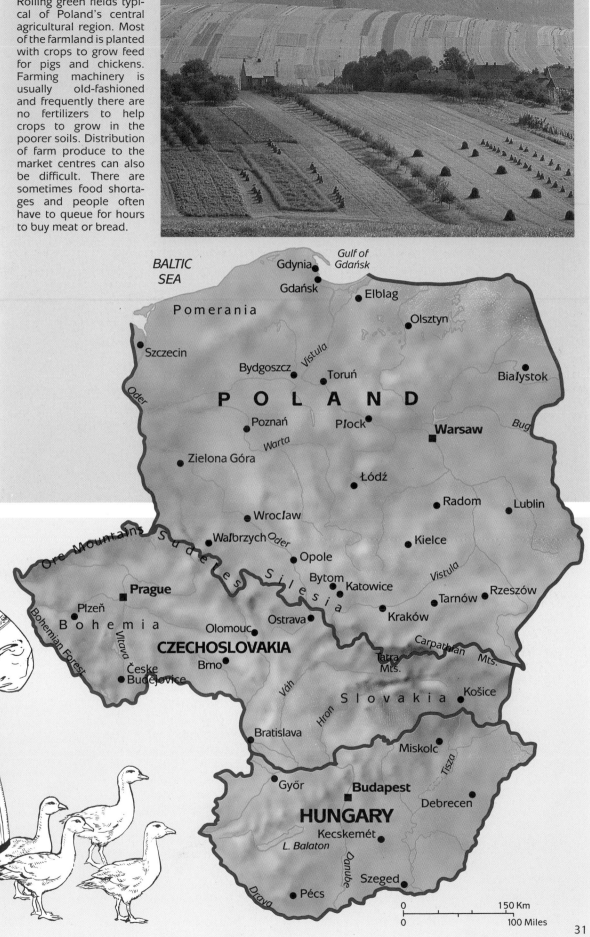

BALTIC SEA

Gulf of Gdańsk

Gdynia

Gdańsk

Elblag

Pomerania

Olsztyn

Szczecin

Bydgoszcz

Toruń

Białystok

Vistula

Oder

P O L A N D

Poznań

Płock

Warsaw

Bug

Warta

Zielona Góra

Łódź

Radom

Lublin

Wrocław

Wałbrzych

Oder

Kielce

Ore Mountains

Sudetes

Opole

Silesia

Bytom

Katowice

Vistula

Rzeszów

Prague

Plzeň

Tarnów

Ostrava

Kraków

Bohemia

Olomouc

Bohemian Forest

Vltava

CZECHOSLOVAKIA

Brno

Carpathian Mts.

Tatra Mts.

České Budějovice

Váh

Slovakia

Košice

Hron

Bratislava

Miskolc

Győr

Budapest

Debrecen

Tisza

HUNGARY

Kecskemét

L. Balaton

Danube

Drava

Szeged

Pécs

| 0 | | 150 Km |
| 0 | | 100 Miles |

31

FORMER SOVIET UNION

In December of 1991 the Union of Soviet Socialist Republics (U.S.S.R.) ceased to exist as a single country. Formed after the Russian Revolution of 1917, it was made up of 15 separate republics. These have now become independent countries, 11 of which agreed to form the Commonwealth of Independent States.

Russia, the largest new country, is also the largest country in the world, stretching across the globe from Europe in the west to the Pacific Ocean in the east. The Ural Mountains, running north to south, divide the country into a European part and an Asian part. Thirty-eight national minorities make up about 20 percent of the non-Russian population of the area that was the U.S.S.R.

cont. page 34

Christians attend a Russian Orthodox service in Moscow.

32

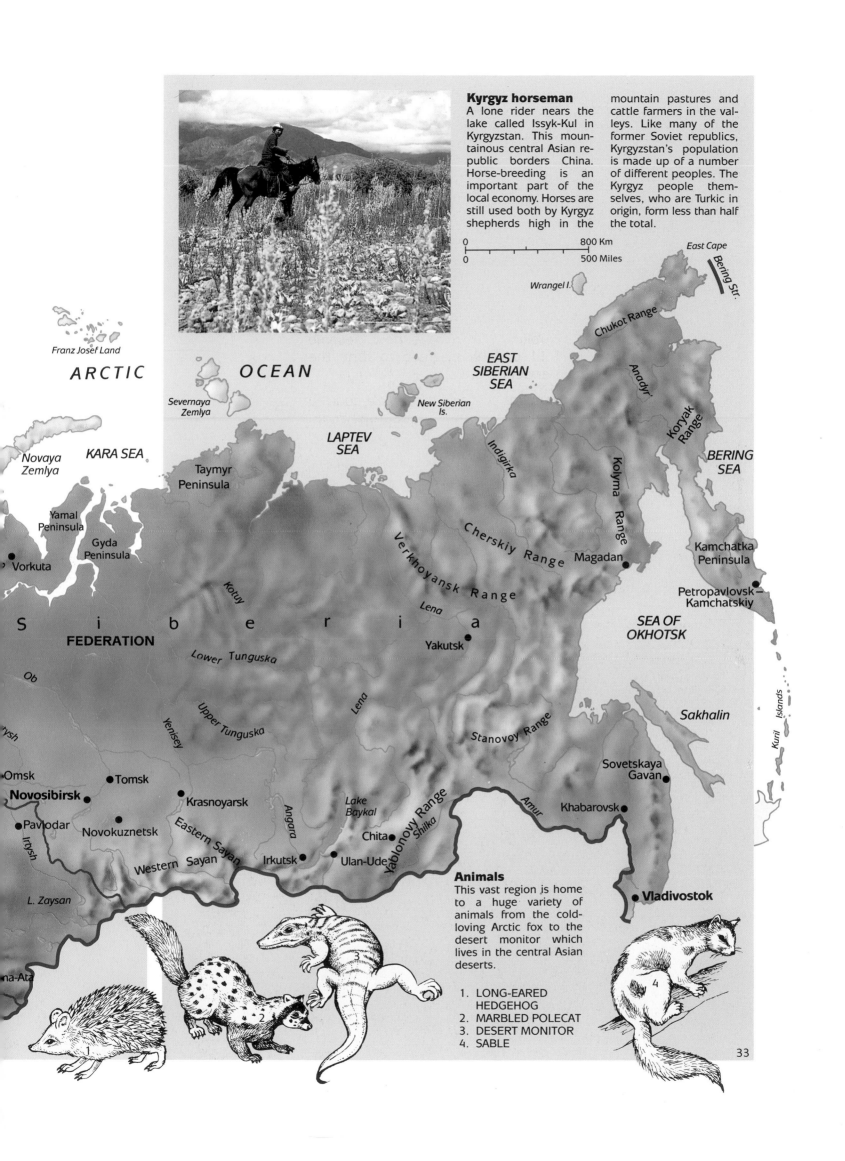

Kyrgyz horseman
A lone rider nears the lake called Issyk-Kul in Kyrgyzstan. This mountainous central Asian republic borders China. Horse-breeding is an important part of the local economy. Horses are still used both by Kyrgyz shepherds high in the mountain pastures and cattle farmers in the valleys. Like many of the former Soviet republics, Kyrgyzstan's population is made up of a number of different peoples. The Kyrgyz people themselves, who are Turkic in origin, form less than half the total.

0   800 Km
0   500 Miles

East Cape

Wrangel I.

Bering Str.

Franz Josef Land

ARCTIC   OCEAN

EAST SIBERIAN SEA

New Siberian Is.

Chukot Range

Severnaya Zemlya

LAPTEV SEA

Anadyr'

Koryak Range

Novaya Zemlya

KARA SEA

Indigirka

Kolyma Range

BERING SEA

Taymyr Peninsula

Yamal Peninsula

Gyda Peninsula

Cherskiy Range

Magadan

Kamchatka Peninsula

● Vorkuta

Verkhoyansk Range

Petropavlovsk–Kamchatskiy

Kotuy

Lena

S i   b   e   r   i   a

FEDERATION

Lower Tunguska

Yakutsk

SEA OF OKHOTSK

Ob

Yenisey

Upper Tunguska

Lena

Sakhalin

Irtysh

Stanovoy Range

● Omsk   ● Tomsk

Sovetskaya Gavan

Novosibirsk ●

Krasnoyarsk

Angara

Lake Baykal

Amur

Khabarovsk ●

Kuril Islands

● Pavlodar

Novokuznetsk

Eastern Sayan

Yablonovy Range

Shilka

Chita

Western Sayan

Irkutsk ●   Ulan-Ude

L. Zaysan

Animals
This vast region is home to a huge variety of animals from the cold-loving Arctic fox to the desert monitor which lives in the central Asian deserts.

● **Vladivostok**

na-Ata

1. LONG-EARED HEDGEHOG
2. MARBLED POLECAT
3. DESERT MONITOR
4. SABLE

33

Winter in the northern city of St. Petersburg is long and cold.

The European countries are the most densely populated and contain well-developed heavy industries, such as coalmining and steel manufacturing. The steel provides raw material for the manufacturing industries around Moscow and the shipbuilding industry in St. Petersburg. In the southern republics, agriculture is more dominant. Ukraine and Kazakhstan contain major grain-growing areas. However, massive amounts of food still have to be imported in order to feed their populations.

Russia's vast eastern region is sparsely populated, but has valuable resources of gas, coal, and oil. However, the inhospitable terrain makes these resources difficult to tap. Another important energy resource is hydroelectric power from the Volga River. This river, the longest in Europe, provides transportation for both people and materials. The Trans-Siberian Railway, which connects Moscow with the Pacific coast many thousands of miles to the east, is also a vital communication link.

The Moscow Metro

The Moscow Metro is the most elegant underground railway system in the world. There are 123 underground stations, all beautifully designed and decorated. There is no graffiti and the stations and trains are spotlessly clean, despite the 10 million people travelling along the 203 kilometres of track each day.

Heavy industries

Manufacturing plants, like this factory which makes lorries and tractors, are located in the major industrial regions in the west of what was once the U.S.S.R. The heavy industries produce one fifth of the world's total industrial output. Raw materials are abundant: the former U.S.S.R. had half the world's iron ore reserves and produced more steel than any other country. Since large areas of arid land have now been irrigated, making it possible to grow extra crops, there is a great demand for agricultural machinery.

34

FORMER SOVIET REPUBLICS

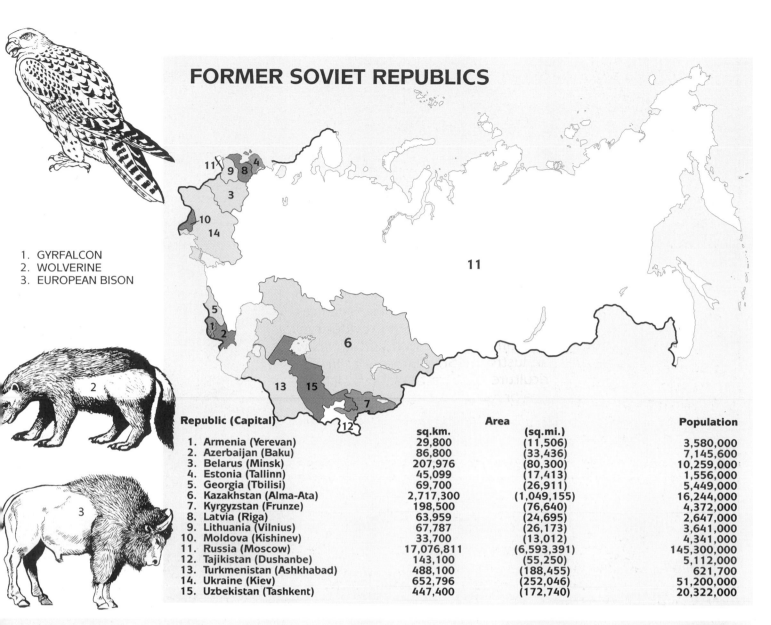

1. GYRFALCON
2. WOLVERINE
3. EUROPEAN BISON

Republic (Capital)	Area		Population
	sq.km.	(sq.mi.)	
1. Armenia (Yerevan)	29,800	(11,506)	3,580,000
2. Azerbaijan (Baku)	86,800	(33,436)	7,145,600
3. Belarus (Minsk)	207,976	(80,300)	10,259,000
4. Estonia (Tallinn)	45,099	(17,413)	1,556,000
5. Georgia (Tbilisi)	69,700	(26,911)	5,449,000
6. Kazakhstan (Alma-Ata)	2,717,300	(1,049,155)	16,244,000
7. Kyrgyzstan (Frunze)	198,500	(76,640)	4,372,000
8. Latvia (Riga)	63,959	(24,695)	2,647,000
9. Lithuania (Vilnius)	67,787	(26,173)	3,641,000
10. Moldova (Kishinev)	33,700	(13,012)	4,341,000
11. Russia (Moscow)	17,076,811	(6,593,391)	145,300,000
12. Tajikistan (Dushanbe)	143,100	(55,250)	5,112,000
13. Turkmenistan (Ashkhabad)	488,100	(188,455)	621,700
14. Ukraine (Kiev)	652,796	(252,046)	51,200,000
15. Uzbekistan (Tashkent)	447,400	(172,740)	20,322,000

Russian ballet

Members of the Bolshoi Ballet performing *Giselle*. Russian ballet is world famous and steeped in tradition. Some of the world's greatest ballets have come from Russia including works such as *Swan Lake*, *The Nutcracker*, and *Sleeping Beauty*. The country has also produced some of the world's best dancers, such as Anna Pavlova and Rudolf Nureyev. Both the Bolshoi, based in Moscow, and the St. Petersburg Ballet are among the world's best companies.

Shopping in a bazaar

Shopping scenes like this bazaar are a common sight in the new Central Asian republics. Open bazaars sell all kinds of items from bowls and baskets to lamps and rugs.

People also shop in open markets where surplus homegrown produce is sold. These are very popular; the food is fresher, though the price is often higher than in the shops.

As the old Soviet economy collapsed, supplies of food became erratic — commodities in abundance one day became scarce on other occasions, sometimes for long periods.

NORTH AMERICA

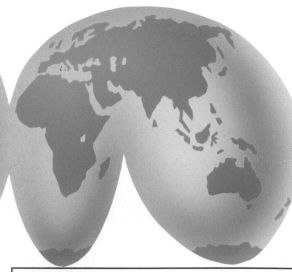

North America stretches from the Arctic icecap to the tropical shores of the Caribbean Sea. It includes two of the largest countries in the world, the United States and Canada, and some of the smallest, the tiny island nations of the West Indies. From Vancouver to St John's, Newfoundland, the continent measures 5000 kilometres across.

The immensely varied landscape includes the tundra and forests of northern Canada, the vast, featureless croplands of the American Midwest, the deserts of northern Mexico and the rainforests of Central America. Running the length of its western side is North America's mountainous backbone. In this region lie the spectacular peaks of the Rocky Mountains, the Grand Canyon and, in Central America, the active volcanoes of Guatemala, El Salvador and Nicaragua.

The Niagara Falls, which lie between Lake Erie and Lake Ontario.

North America
Highest point Mount McKinley (Alaska, USA) 6194m. (20,320ft.)
Lowest point Death Valley (California, USA) 86m. (282ft.)
Longest river Mississippi-Missouri-Red Rock (USA) 5970 km. (3710mi.)
Largest lake Superior (USA/Canada) 82,348 sq.km. (31,795 sq.mi.).

UNITED STATES OF AMERICA
Area 9,372,570 sq. km. (3,618,700 sq. miles)
Population 247,410,000
Capital Washington D.C. (pop. 638,432)
Largest cities New York (7,262,700)
Los Angeles (3,259,340)
Chicago (3,009,530)
Houston (1,728,910)
Philadelphia (1,642,900)
Detroit (1,086,220)
San Diego (1,015,190)
Dallas (1,003,520)
Currency US dollar
Official language(s) English (Spanish is also spoken)
Chief products Wheat, maize, soya beans, minerals, machinery, oil, natural gas, iron and steel
Exports Machinery, vehicles, cereals, chemicals, crude materials
Imports Machinery, vehicles, manufactured goods, petroleum, food (fish and vegetables) oil

CANADA
Area 9,976,139 sq. km. (3,851,810 sq. miles)
Population 25,895,000
Capital Ottawa (pop. 300,763)
Largest cities Toronto (3,427,168)
Montreal (2,921,357)
Vancouver (1,380,729)
Edmonton (785,465)
Calgary (671,326)
Currency Canadian dollar
Official language(s) English and French
Chief products Wheat, minerals, furs, timber, fish, oil, natural gas
Exports Machinery, paper, vehicles, timber, metals (especially aluminium, nickel, uranium)
Imports Machinery, food, vehicles, chemicals, iron and steel, petroleum

GREENLAND (Denmark)
Area 2,175,601 sq. km. (840,004 sq. miles)
Population 53,406
Capital Godthåb

MEXICO
Official name Estados Unidos Mexicanos
Area 1,972,547 sq. km. (761,610 sq. miles)
Population 85,300,000
Capital Mexico City (pop. 18,748,000)
Largest cities Guadalajara (2,578,000)
Monterrey (2,335,000)
Puebla (1,217,600),
León (946,800)
Torreón (729,800)
Currency Mexican peso
Official language(s) Spanish (Amerindian languages are also spoken)
Chief products Oil, iron and steel, minerals (especially gold and silver), maize, sorghum, oranges
Exports Oil, manufactured goods, machinery, minerals, textiles, coffee
Imports Vehicles, industrial machinery (motor pumps, textile machinery), food (maize and soya beans)

GUATEMALA
Area 108,889 sq. km. (42,040 sq. miles)
Population 8,818,000
Capital Guatemala City
Chief products Coffee, cotton, chemicals, bananas, maize, sugar cane

EL SALVADOR
Area 21,041 sq. km. (8120 sq. miles)
Population 5,122,000
Capital San Salvador
Chief products Coffee, textiles, sugar cane, maize

NICARAGUA
Area 148,000 sq. km. (57,130 sq. miles)
Population 3,689,000
Capital Managua
Chief products Coffee, cotton, sugar, shellfish

COSTA RICA
Area 50,700 sq. km. (19,600 sq. miles)
Population 2,990,000
Capital San José
Chief products Coffee, bananas, sugar, cocoa, cattle, manufactured goods

NAME	AREA SQ. KM. (SQ. MILES)	POPULATION	CAPITAL
Anguilla (UK)	91 (35)	7000	The Valley
Antigua and Barbuda	442 (171)	81,000	St John's
Aruba (Netherlands)	193 (75)	68,000	Oranjestad
Bahamas	13,864 (5353)	243,000	Nassau
Barbados	430 (166)	250,000	Bridgetown
Bermuda (UK)	54 (21)	57,145	Hamilton
British Virgin Islands (UK)	153 (59)	12,000	Road Town
Cayman Islands (UK)	259 (100)	22,000	Georgetown
Dominica	752 (290)	77,000	Roseau
Grenada	345 (133)	112,000	St George's
Guadeloupe (Fr)	1702 (657)	330,000	Basse-Terre
Martinique (Fr)	1079 (417)	330,000	Fort-de-France
Montserrat (UK)	106 (41)	12,000	Plymouth
Netherlands Antilles (Netherlands)	993 (383)	261,850	Willemstad
St Christopher (Kitts)-Nevis	262 (101)	46,000	Basseterre
St Lucia	616 (238)	132,000	Castries
St Vincent and the Grenadines	388 (150)	100,000	Kingstown
Trinidad and Tobago	5130 (1980)	1,204,000	Port of Spain
Turks and Caicos Is. (UK)	430 (192)	8000	Coburn Town
US Virgin Islands (USA)	345 (133)	111,000	Charlotte Amalie
St Pierre et Miquelon (Fr)	241 (93)	6500	St Pierre

ANTIGUA AND BARBUDA

BAHAMAS

BARBADOS

DOMINICA

GRENADA

ST CHRISTOPHER (KITTS)-NEVIS

ST LUCIA

ST VINCENT AND THE GRENADINES

TRINIDAD AND TOBAGO

US VIRGIN ISLANDS

JAMAICA
Area 10,991 sq. km. (4,240 sq. miles)
Population 2,470,000
Capital Kingston
Chief products Sugar, bananas, alumina, bauxite

HAITI
Area 27,750 sq. km. (10,710 sq. miles)
Population 5,358,000
Capital Port-au-Prince
Chief products Coffee, sisal, manufactured goods, sugar

DOMINICAN REPUBLIC
Area 48,374 sq. km. (18,820 sq. miles)
Population 6,416,000
Capital Santo Domingo
Chief products Sugar, bauxite, silver, cocoa, coffee

Greenland (Denmark)

BELIZE
Area 22,963 sq. km. (8,870 sq. miles)
Population 184,000
Capital Belmopan
Chief products Fruit, fish, vegetables, shellfish, timber

HONDURAS
Area 112,088 sq. km. (43,280 sq. miles)
Population 5,047,000
Capital Tegucigalpa
Chief products Bananas, coffee, timber, sugar, tobacco

PANAMA
Area 77,082 sq. km. (29,670 sq. miles)
Population 2,346,000
Capital Panama
Chief products Bananas, timber, copper, rice, sugar

PUERTO RICO (USA)
Area 9104 sq. km. (3520 sq. miles)
Population 3,301,000
Capital San Juan
Chief products Manufactured goods, sugar cane, machinery, coffee

CUBA
Area 110,861 sq. km. (42,800 sq. miles)
Population 10,440,000
Capital Havana
Chief products Sugar, oil, minerals (nickel, iron ore), rice, maize, coffee, tobacco

Alaska (U.S.)

C A N A D A

UNITED STATES OF AMERICA

Saint Pierre and Miquelon (Fr.)

Bermuda (Br.)

MEXICO

BAHAMAS

CUBA

Puerto Rico (U.S.)

ANTIGUA & BARBUDA

DOMINICAN REPUBLIC

HAITI

JAMAICA

DOMINICA

ST. LUCIA

ST. VINCENT

GRENADA

BARBADOS

TRINIDAD & TOBAGO

BELIZE

GUATEMALA

HONDURAS

EL SALVADOR

NICARAGUA

PANAMA

COSTA RICA

CANADA

Canada is the second largest country in the world, yet nearly ninety per cent of it is uninhabited. Much of its territory is either mountainous 'tundra' (Arctic plains where the soil is permanently frozen) or forested. Most of the people live in the cities that hug the Great Lakes and the St Lawrence Seaway, a major route taking ships inland.

Canada has rich natural resources of minerals such as zinc, nickel and uranium. Furniture and paper are made from the huge supplies of wood, while vast prairie lands make Canada one of the world's leading producers of wheat. Fishing is important on the Atlantic coast off Newfoundland: shellfish, lobsters and cod are canned or frozen for export.

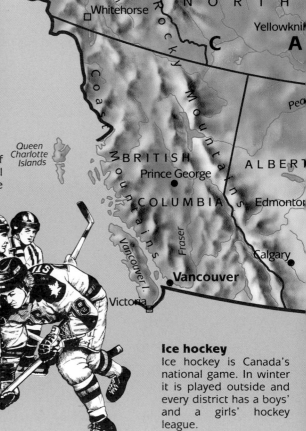

The Welland Canal
The Welland Canal connects two of the Great Lakes, Erie and Ontario.

It is deep enough for container ships, bound for the Atlantic Ocean via the St Lawrence Seaway.

The Prairies
The vast fertile plains of Saskatchewan in central Canada are known as 'the Prairies'.

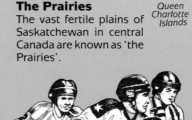
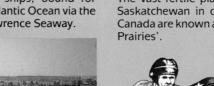

Ice hockey
Ice hockey is Canada's national game. In winter it is played outside and every district has a boys' and a girls' hockey league.

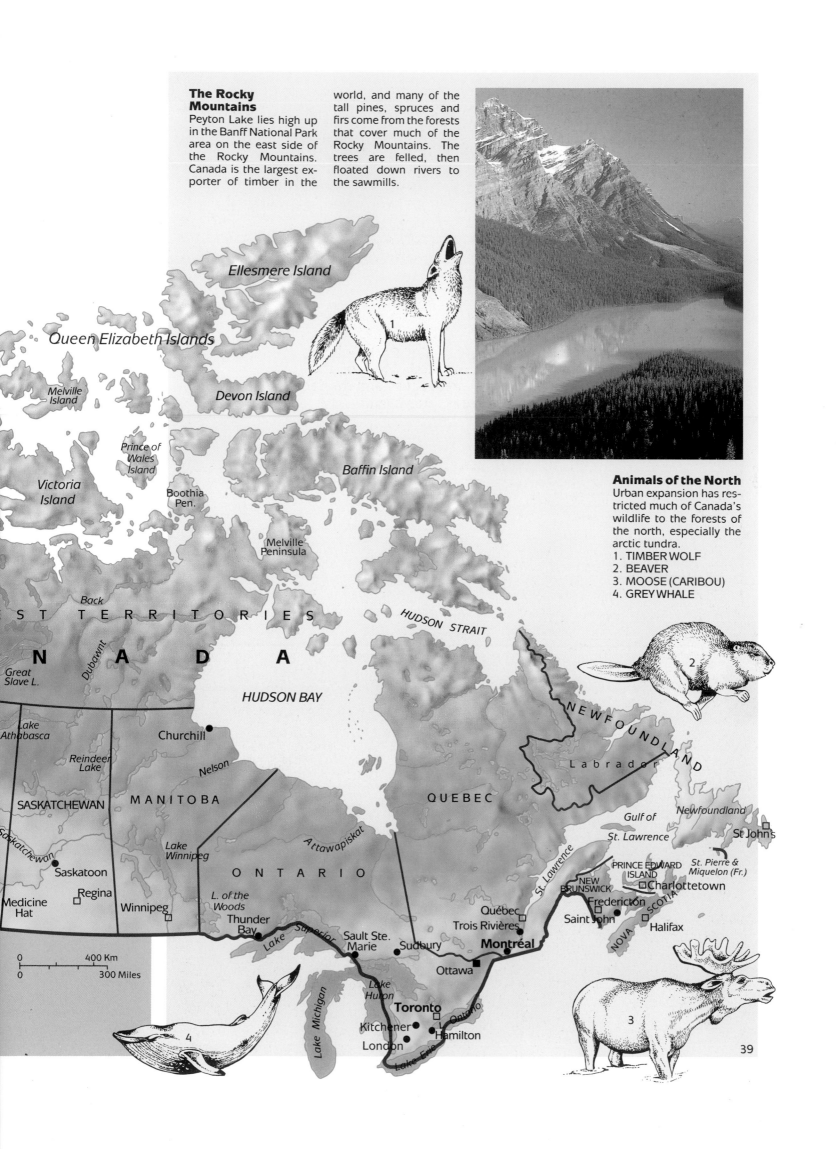

The Rocky Mountains

Peyton Lake lies high up in the Banff National Park area on the east side of the Rocky Mountains. Canada is the largest exporter of timber in the world, and many of the tall pines, spruces and firs come from the forests that cover much of the Rocky Mountains. The trees are felled, then floated down rivers to the sawmills.

Animals of the North

Urban expansion has restricted much of Canada's wildlife to the forests of the north, especially the arctic tundra.
1. TIMBER WOLF
2. BEAVER
3. MOOSE (CARIBOU)
4. GREY WHALE

Ellesmere Island

Queen Elizabeth Islands

Melville Island

Devon Island

Victoria Island

Prince of Wales Island

Boothia Pen.

Baffin Island

Melville Peninsula

Back

ST TERRITORIES

Great Slave L.

Dubawnt

NADA

HUDSON STRAIT

HUDSON BAY

Lake Athabasca

Churchill

Reindeer Lake

Nelson

NEWFOUNDLAND

Labrador

SASKATCHEWAN

MANITOBA

QUEBEC

Saskatchewan

Attawapiskat

Lake Winnipeg

Gulf of St. Lawrence

Newfoundland

St John's

Saskatoon

ONTARIO

St. Lawrence

PRINCE EDWARD ISLAND

St. Pierre & Miquelon (Fr.)

Regina

L. of the Woods

NEW BRUNSWICK

Charlottetown

Medicine Hat

Winnipeg

Thunder Bay

Lake Superior

Sault Ste. Marie

Sudbury

Québec

Trois Rivières

Fredericton

Saint John

NOVA SCOTIA

Halifax

Montréal

| 0 | 400 Km |
| 0 | 300 Miles |

Ottawa

Lake Michigan

Lake Huron

Toronto

L. Ontario

Kitchener

Hamilton

London

Lake Erie

39

UNITED STATES OF AMERICA

The USA is the fourth largest country in the world. It is made up of 50 states, 48 of which lie between Canada and Mexico. The other two are the islands of Hawaii in the Pacific Ocean, and Alaska in the north-western corner of North America, which was bought from the Russians in 1867.

The USA is a country of huge natural resources. Between the Rocky Mountains in the west and the Appalachian Mountains in the east lie huge areas of prairie land where maize, wheat, soya beans and many other crops are grown on highly-mechanized farms. Despite large reserves of oil in Alaska, the USA is such a huge consumer that it still has to import stocks of oil.

cont. page 42

Kauai

Niihau
Kaula

Kauai Channel

Oahu

Honolulu

Kaiwi Channel

Molokai

Lanai

Maui

Kahoolawe

Alenuihana Channel

Hawaiian Islands

PACIFIC OCEAN

HAWAII

Mauna Kea
4205

Hilo

Hawaii

Mauna Loa
4169

0   150 Kms

0   100 Miles

C. Flattery

Seattle

Olympia

Mt. Rainier   WASHINGTON
4392

Portland

Salem

Great Falls

Helena

M O N

Boise

I D A H O

Yellow
Nation

Coast Range

Cascade Range

OREGON

Snake

Sacramento

Oakland

San Francisco

Great
Basin

Carson City

NEVADA

Great
Salt
Lake

Salt Lake
City

U T A H

Coast Range

Mt Whitney
4418

Las Vegas

Grand
Canyon

Colorado

Los Angeles
Long Beach

San Diego

A R I Z O N A

Gila

Phoenix

Tucson

Bryce Canyon, Utah
Bryce Canyon is about 150 kilometres north of the Grand Canyon. Centuries of erosion from wind and frost have produced this spectacle of brilliantly coloured spires. The canyon is a large U-shaped amphitheatre, one and a half kilometres wide.

Wildlife in the USA
Three animals from the great variety of wildlife in the USA.
1. CALIFORNIA SEALION
2. RACCOON
3. BALD EAGLE

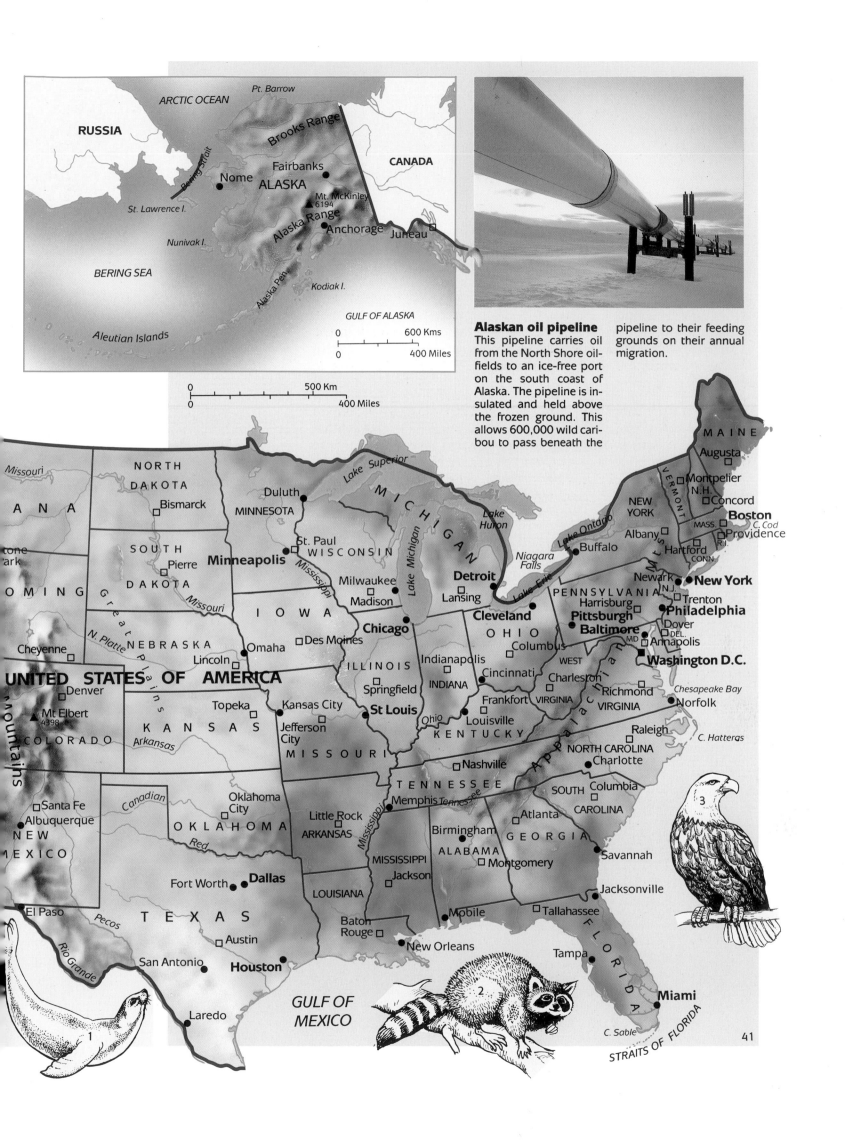

ARCTIC OCEAN

Pt. Barrow

RUSSIA

Brooks Range

CANADA

Bering Strait

Nome

Fairbanks

ALASKA

St. Lawrence I.

Mt. McKinley
6194

Alaska Range

Nunivak I.

Anchorage

Juneau

BERING SEA

Kodiak I.

Alaska Pen.

GULF OF ALASKA

Aleutian Islands

0   600 Kms

0   400 Miles

Alaskan oil pipeline
This pipeline carries oil from the North Shore oilfields to an ice-free port on the south coast of Alaska. The pipeline is insulated and held above the frozen ground. This allows 600,000 wild caribou to pass beneath the pipeline to their feeding grounds on their annual migration.

0   500 Km

0   400 Miles

Missouri

NORTH DAKOTA

Bismarck

Duluth

MINNESOTA

Lake Superior

MICHIGAN

MAINE

Augusta

ANA

one ark

SOUTH DAKOTA

Pierre

St. Paul

WISCONSIN

Minneapolis

Mississippi

Milwaukee

Madison

Lake Michigan

Lake Huron

MICHIGAN

Lansing

Lake Ontario

Niagara Falls

Buffalo

Lake Erie

Montpelier

N.H.

VERMONT

NEW YORK

Concord

Boston

C. Cod

Albany

MASS.

Providence

Hartford

R.I.

CONN.

OMING

Missouri

IOWA

Detroit

Cleveland

PENNSYLVANIA

Newark

New York

N.J.

Trenton

Harrisburg

Pittsburgh

Philadelphia

UNITED STATES OF AMERICA

Great Plains

N. Platte

Cheyenne

Denver

Mt Elbert
4398

COLORADO

ountains

NEBRASKA

Omaha

Lincoln

Des Moines

Chicago

ILLINOIS

Springfield

INDIANA

Indianapolis

OHIO

Columbus

Cincinnati

WEST VIRGINIA

Charleston

Frankfort

VIRGINIA

Dover

DEL.

Baltimore

MD

Annapolis

Washington D.C.

Richmond

VIRGINIA

Chesapeake Bay

Norfolk

Topeka

Kansas City

St Louis

KANSAS

Jefferson City

Arkansas

MISSOURI

Louisville

Ohio

KENTUCKY

Nashville

Raleigh

C. Hatteras

NORTH CAROLINA

Charlotte

Santa Fe

Albuquerque

NEW MEXICO

Canadian

Oklahoma City

OKLAHOMA

Red

Little Rock

ARKANSAS

TENNESSEE

Memphis

Tennessee

Mississippi

Birmingham

MISSISSIPPI

Jackson

ALABAMA

Montgomery

GEORGIA

Atlanta

SOUTH CAROLINA

Columbia

Savannah

Appalachian

El Paso

Pecos

TEXAS

Fort Worth

Dallas

Austin

San Antonio

Houston

LOUISIANA

Baton Rouge

Mobile

Tallahassee

Jacksonville

FLORIDA

Rio Grande

Laredo

GULF OF MEXICO

New Orleans

Tampa

Miami

C. Sable

STRAITS OF FLORIDA

1

2

3

41

Heavy industry is concentrated in the north-east and around the Great Lakes, but more recently high-tech and light industry has developed in the west, especially in the states of Texas and California, which are now the biggest manufacturing states in the USA.

People have come from every continent to live in the USA. Many of the few surviving native Americans live on areas set aside for them called 'Indian Reserves'. The first black peoples were brought by the Europeans from West Africa, and forced to work on the plantations in the south as slaves. Huge numbers of Jews and other Europeans arrived in the late nineteenth century, seeking a better life.

The USA is famous for many things: its space technology which put the first man on the moon, Ford Motors – the biggest car and truck manufacturer in the world, New York with its skyscrapers and important business centre, the film industry in Hollywood in California, and its beautiful National Parks such as the Grand Canyon and Yellowstone.

Navajo Indians
The Navajo is the largest Indian tribe in the USA.

Most of the Indians live on a reservation in the west.

Farming in South California
These men are loading lettuces on to a truck. California, on the west coast of the USA, sells a greater value of farm products than any other state. Particular areas of California specialize in particular crops – in the north of the state citrus fruits and vines are cultivated.

Pittsburgh (top)
Pittsburgh is one of the centres of heavy manufacturing in the northern USA with large iron and steel and chemical works.

42

State	Capital	Population
1. Alabama	Montgomery	4,053,000
2. Alaska	Juneau	534,000
3. Arizona	Phoenix	3,317,000
4. Arkansas	Little Rock	2,372,000
5. California	Sacramento	26,981,000
6. Colorado	Denver	3,267,000
7. Connecticut	Hartford	3,189,000
8. Delaware	Dover	633,000
9. Florida	Tallahassee	11,675,000
10. Georgia	Atlanta	5,975,000
11. Hawaii	Honolulu	1,062,000
12. Idaho	Boise	1,003,000
13. Illinois	Springfield	11,553,000
14. Indiana	Indianapolis	5,504,000
15. Iowa	Des Moines	2,851,000
16. Kansas	Topeka	2,461,000
17. Kentucky	Frankfort	3,728,000
18. Louisiana	Baton Rouge	4,501,000
19. Maine	Augusta	1,174,000
20. Maryland	Annapolis	4,463,000
21. Massachusetts	Boston	5,832,000
22. Michigan	Lansing	9,145,000
23. Minnesota	St Paul	4,214,000
24. Mississippi	Jackson	2,625,000
25. Missouri	Jefferson City	5,066,000
26. Montana	Helena	819,000
27. Nebraska	Lincoln	1,598,000
28. Nevada	Carson City	963,000
29. New Hampshire	Concord	1,027,000
30. New Jersey	Trenton	7,620,000
31. New Mexico	Santa Fe	1,479,000
32. New York	Albany	17,772,000
33. North Carolina	Raleigh	6,331,000
34. North Dakota	Bismarck	679,000
35. Ohio	Columbus	10,752,000
36. Oklahoma	Oklahoma City	3,305,000
37. Oregon	Salem	2,698,000
38. Pennsylvania	Harrisburg	11,889,000
39. Rhode Island	Providence	975,000
40. South Carolina	Columbia	3,378,000
41. South Dakota	Pierre	708,000
42. Tennessee	Nashville	4,803,000
43. Texas	Austin	16,682,000
44. Utah	Salt Lake City	1,665,000
45. Vermont	Montpelier	541,000
46. Virginia	Richmond	5,787,000
47. Washington	Olympia	4,463,000
48. West Virginia	Charleston	1,919,000
49. Wisconsin	Madison	4,785,000
50. Wyoming	Cheyenne	507,000

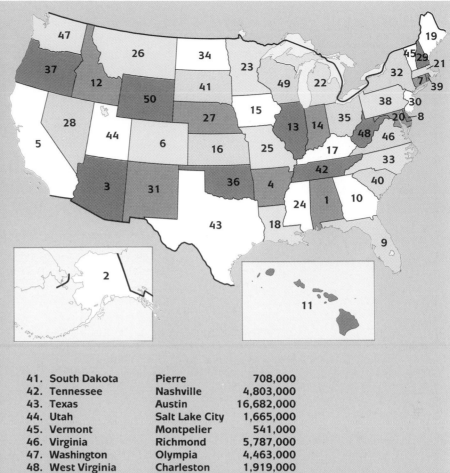

The District of Columbia, including the capital, Washington DC, is not a state — it is administered directly by Congress.

Jazz band, New Orleans

The first jazz bands started in the city of New Orleans in the south of the USA. The 'Great Age' of jazz was in the 1920s when New Orleans was a colourful and cosmopolitan city. Groups of black musicians would play together spontaneously and new styles of dancing developed. An annual jazz festival is still celebrated called the 'Mardi Gras'. Much of today's pop music originated from jazz.

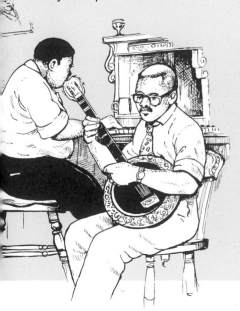

New Hampshire in the Autumn

The far north-eastern corner of the USA, known as New England, is renowned for the colours of the leaves in autumn. Outdoor sports such as fishing, hunting and grouse-shooting are very popular in the unspoilt countryside. This is the land of the first settlers from Britain in the early seventeenth century, and many of the place names are derived from towns and villages in England.

CENTRAL AMERICA AND MEXICO

Mexico and the other Central American countries – Guatemala, Nicaragua, El Salvador, Honduras, Belize, Costa Rica and Panama – form a long land bridge joining North and South America. Mexico is the largest of these countries – in fact more people live in its capital, Mexico City, than in any of the other Central American states.

The people of Central America are descended from the original Indian tribes that inhabited the area, and from the Spanish who arrived in the sixteenth century. Many people are of mixed Indian and Spanish blood and are known as *mestizos*.

Mexico has valuable natural reserves of gold and silver, and large oil fields in the Gulf of Mexico. The other Central American countries are poorer, relying heavily on the export of crops such as cotton, bananas and sugar, and many are torn by civil war.

Tijuana
Mexicali
Ciudad Juárez
Lower California
Gulf of California
Hermosillo
Sierra Madre
California
M E
Culiacán
Mazatlá
C. San Lucas

A market in Xochimilco, Mexico
This woman is weaving a traditional rug at a market. Hand-weaving is an ancient Indian art that is still practised, especially in the south where there is a larger native Indian population. Styles vary according to region so that the region which an Indian comes from can be identified by the colours and patterns on their clothes and rugs.

44

Cacti in the Mexican desert

The cactus plant is often the only form of life in the deserts of northern Mexico. Some years there is no rain at all, especially in Lower California. However, there are hundreds of different species of cacti, and some yield juices which are turned into alcoholic drinks. One of these drinks is called tequila which is used to make cocktails. Plantations are now run to produce tequila for export, as it has become popular around the world. A stronger and cheaper drink, which has been made since the days of the Mayans, is pulque, known as the poor Mexican's beer. The juice is squeezed from the fleshy leaves of a very tall variety of cactus, often taller than a person.

The Panama Canal

The Panama Canal is one of the greatest feats of engineering in the world. It is 65 kilometres long, and was built so that ships could pass between the Atlantic and Pacific Oceans without having to sail south around South America. This involved hacking out kilometres of rock, damming rivers and building huge iron locks. It was completed by the USA but is now jointly administered by the USA and Panama. The canal is very important to world trade and shipping companies have to pay a high toll to the Panamanian government for its use. The canal brings many jobs for the local people.

Cutting bananas

The banana is one of the most important crops grown in the countries of Central America. Machete knives are used to cut the clumps of bananas while they are still green. They are then exported to the USA and Europe in time for them to ripen just before delivery to the shops.

hihuahua

Río Grande

Nuevo Laredo

MEXICO

Sierra Madre Oriental

Torreón
Saltillo
Matamoros
Monterrey

Occidental

R. Grande de Santiago

San Luis Potosí
Tampico

Aguascalientes

León
Querétaro

adalajara

Morelia
Mexico City
Veracruz

Cuernavaca
Puebla ▲ Citlaltepetl
5700
Balsas
Orizaba

Acapulco

Oaxaca

Isthmus of Tehuantepec
Minatitlán

GULF OF MEXICO

Gulf of Campeche

Mérida

Yucatán

I. de Cozumel

Belize City
Belmopan
BELIZE

Gulf of Tehuantepec

GUATEMALA
Guatemala City

San Salvador

EL SALVADOR

Tegucigalpa

HONDURAS

C. Gracias á Dios

Mosquito Coast

NICARAGUA

Managua

L. Nicaragua

PACIFIC OCEAN

COSTA RICA
San José

Panama Canal
Panama

PANAMA

Gulf of Panama

0   500 Km

0   400 Miles

CARIBBEAN ISLANDS

The islands of the West Indies lie between North and South America. Commonly known as the Caribbean, this region contains 24 countries whose populations range in size from a few thousand to over 10 million, and whose people speak five main languages as well as many other local dialects.

Today over half of the countries of the Caribbean are politically independent; others, such as the British Virgin Islands and Guadeloupe, are still colonies. The wealth of the Caribbean countries varies immensely. Bermuda and the Cayman Islands both have thriving tourist industries and are important financial centres. In contrast, Haiti is one of the poorest countries in the western hemisphere.

The tropical climate of this region is especially suited to growing sugar cane, which is used to produce sugar, molasses (a kind of syrup) and rum for export. Other crops include coffee, tobacco, cacao (to make chocolate and cocoa) and citrus fruits.

GULF OF MEXICO

Straits of Florida

Havana
Santa Clara
Cienfueg
I. de Juventud

Cayman Is.
Grand Cayman (Br.)
(Br.)

Cutting sugar cane in Cuba

Sugar cane is Cuba's most valuable crop. It makes up eighty per cent of its exports, most of which go to the USSR and Eastern Europe. Long machete knives are used to cut down the cane, which is then taken to the sugar mills for processing. The cane is ground in the mill and boiled in water until sugar crystals are formed. Cuba is one of the top three sugar producers in the world.

Festival time

Music can be heard everywhere at carnival time in the Caribbean. People dress in traditional costumes and dance in the streets. This is the home of reggae music, and calypso songs. The musical instruments are usually home-made: drums from hollow logs, and shakers from dried shells.

Hamilton ● *Bermuda (Br.)*

Curaçao

Many of the Caribbean islands show the influence of the European settlers in the past. Curaçao was first occupied by the Spanish and then by the Dutch. Many of its buildings today — churches, halls, schools and houses — were erected by the colonists. The main language spoken on Curaçao is Dutch, though there is also a popular tongue spoken throughout the Caribbean which is called Creole. This developed from the earliest contacts between Europeans and Africans who were brought to the island as slaves.

Bartering for fish

Fish is often sold straight from the boat in the Caribbean. Local fishers sail up the busy quayside, where in some places there are floating markets. Everybody gathers round to see the fresh catch and the bartering begins. The people shout out offers for particular pieces of fish, depending on the type and size. There is a rich diversity of fish in the Caribbean Sea and it is the main food eaten on the islands.

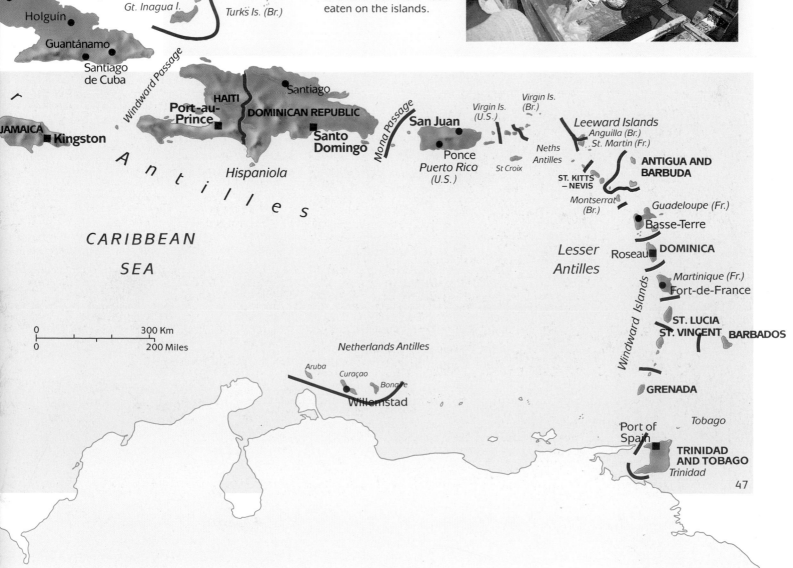

Gt. Abaco I.
nama I.

New Providence I.   *Eleuthera I.*

■ Nassau   **BAHAMAS**

Andros I.   *Cat. I.*

Long I.

CUBA

● Camagüey   *Acklins I.*   *Caicos Is. (Br.)*

● Holguín   *Gt. Inagua I.*   *Turks Is. (Br.)*

● Guantánamo

● Santiago de Cuba

Windward Passage

A n t i l l e s

JAMAICA ■ **Kingston**

HAITI
Port-au-Prince ■   **DOMINICAN REPUBLIC**   ● Santiago

Hispaniola   ■ **Santo Domingo**

Mona Passage

San Juan ■

Ponce ●
Puerto Rico (U.S.)   *St Croix*

Virgin Is. (U.S.)   *Virgin Is. (Br.)*

Leeward Islands
Anguilla (Br.)
St. Martin (Fr.)

Neths Antilles

ST. KITTS – NEVIS

ANTIGUA AND BARBUDA

Montserrat (Br.)

Guadeloupe (Fr.)
● **Basse-Terre**

DOMINICA
Roseau ■

Martinique (Fr.)
● **Fort-de-France**

Lesser Antilles

CARIBBEAN

SEA

Windward Islands

ST. LUCIA
ST. VINCENT   **BARBADOS**

0		300 Km
0		200 Miles

Netherlands Antilles

Aruba
Curaçao   *Bonaire*
Willemstad

● **GRENADA**

Tobago

Port of Spain ■   **TRINIDAD AND TOBAGO**
Trinidad

SOUTH AMERICA

South America stretches from the Caribbean Sea, well above the Equator, down to Cape Horn, the cold southernmost tip which is only 990 kilometres away from Antarctica. It is made up of 13 countries; the largest is Brazil which covers nearly half of the total area of the continent.

The Andes mountains run almost the entire length of South America with peaks up to 7000 metres. Spanning the continent, from its source in the Peruvian Andes through the Brazilian rainforest to the Atlantic Ocean, is the mighty Amazon river, at 6515 kilometres the second longest river in the world. South of the rainforest are the plateau grasslands of the Pampas. To the west of the Andes, squeezed between the coast and the mountains, lies the Atacama Desert, reputedly the driest desert in the world.

The Straits of Magellan in southern Chile.

South America:

Highest point Mount Aconcagua (Argentina) 6960m. (22,834ft.) above sea level
Lowest point Peninsula Valdés (Argentina) 40m. (131ft.) below sea level

Longest river Amazon 6515km. (4050mi.)
Largest lake Titicaca (Peru/Bolivia) 8340 sq.km. (3220 sq.mi.)

ARGENTINA
Official name República Argentina
Area 2,766,889 sq. km. (1,068,302 sq. miles)
Population 31,497,000
Capital Buenos Aires (pop. 2,922,829)
Largest cities Santa Fé (2,465,829)
Córdoba (2,407,754)
Mendoza (1,196,228)
Tucumán (972,655)
Entre Rios (908,313)
Corrientes (661,454)
Currency Austral
Official language(s) Spanish
Chief products Meat products (especially beef and mutton), wool, oil, minerals (coal, lead, zinc and iron ore), natural gas, wine, machine tools, vehicles, textiles, wheat, maize
Exports Meat, cereals, wool
Imports Machinery, iron and steel, non-ferrous metals

BRAZIL
Official name República Federativa do Brasil
Area 8,511,965 sq. km. (3,286,488 sq. miles)
Population 141,452,000
Capital Brasilia (pop. 1,567,709)
Largest cities São Paulo (10,063,110)
Rio de Janeiro (5,603,388)
Belo Horizonte (2,114,429)
Salvador (1,804,438)
Fortaleza (1,582,414)
Nova Iguaçu (1,319,491)
Currency Novo Cruzado
Official language(s) Portuguese (Italian, Spanish, German, Japanese, Arabic are also spoken)
Chief products Iron ore, manganese, bauxite, chrome, diamonds, maize, black beans, cassava, coffee, cotton, soya, rice
Exports Coffee, cotton, iron ore, machinery
Imports Machinery, crude oil, cereals, non-ferrous metals

BOLIVIA
Official name República de Bolivia
Area 1,098,581 sq. km. (424,164 sq. miles)
Population 6,740,417
Capital La Paz (Legal capital – Sucre)
Official language(s) Spanish
Chief products Tin, natural gas, coffee, wood, natural rubber, potatoes, maize

CHILE
Official name República de Chile
Area 756,626 sq. km. (292,132 sq. miles)
Population 12,748,498
Capital Santiago
Official language(s) Spanish
Chief products Copper, nitrate, wheat, livestock, fish, iron ore, timber, vegetables, fruit, silver

COLOMBIA
Official name República de Colombia
Area 1,141,748 sq. km. (440,831 sq. miles)
Population 29,188,000
Capital Bogotá
Official language(s) Spanish
Chief products Coffee, cotton, bananas, tobacco, gold, coal, petroleum, textiles, precious stones

ECUADOR
Official name República del Ecuador
Area 461,475 sq. km. (178,130 sq. miles)
Population 10,203,722
Capital Quito
Official language(s) Spanish
Chief products Bananas, coffee, cocoa, petroleum, rice, fish (especially shrimps and sardines), African palm

Beautiful scenery high in the Andes Mountains.

PERU
Official name República del Perú
Area 1,285,216 sq. km. (496,225 sq. miles)
Population 20,727,000
Capital Lima (pop. 5,008,400)
Largest cities Arequipa (561,338) Iquitos (540,560) Chiclayo (533,266)
Currency Inti
Official language(s) Spanish (Quechua and Aymará are also spoken)
Chief products Fishmeal, iron ore, copper, silver, zinc, lead, sugar, wheat, maize, petroleum, timber, cotton

VENEZUELA
Official name República de Venezuela
Area 912,050 sq. km. (352,144 sq. miles)
Population 18,757,389
Capital Caracas
Official language(s) Spanish
Chief products Oil, petroleum, petro-chemicals, aluminium, plastics, steel products, gold, diamonds, asbestos, textiles

GUYANA
Official name The Co-operative Republic of Guyana
Area 214,969 sq. km. (83,000 sq. miles)
Population 971,000
Capital Georgetown
Official language(s) English
Chief products Sugar, rice, bauxite, alumina, diamonds, gold, timber, rum

VENEZUELA
GUYANA
COLOMBIA
FR. GUIANA
SURINAME
ECUADOR
B R A Z I L
PERU
BOLIVIA
PARAGUAY
C H I L E
URUGUAY
ARGENTINA
Falkland Is. (Br.)

PARAGUAY
Official name República del Paraguay
Area 406,752 sq. km. (157,048 sq. miles)
Population 3,807,000
Capital Asunción
Official language(s) Spanish (Guarini is also spoken)
Chief products Processed meat, cotton, soya beans, tobacco, sugar, coffee, timber

URUGUAY
Official name República Oriental del Uruguay
Area 186,925 sq. km. (72,155 sq. miles)
Population 3,058,000
Capital Montevideo
Official language(s) Spanish
Chief products Wool, meat products, textiles, fish, fruits, wheat, barley, maize, petroleum products

SURINAME
Official name Nieuwe Republiek van Suriname
Area 163,265 sq. km. (63,037 sq. miles)
Population 394,768
Capital Paramaribo
Official language(s) Dutch
Chief products Timber, rice, sugar cane, bauxite

FALKLAND ISLANDS (UK)
Area 12,175 sq. km. (4700 sq. miles)
Population 1919
Capital Port Stanley

FRENCH GUIANA
Official name Guyane
Area 90,000 sq. km. (34,750 sq. miles)
Population 84,180
Capital Cayenne
Official language(s) French (Creole is also spoken)
Chief products Fish, (especially shrimps), hardwood, timber, sugar cane, cayenne pepper

49

NORTHERN SOUTH AMERICA

The landscape of the countries of this region varies from the mountain ranges and plains of the Andes mountains in the west to the tropical rain forests of the north.

Many of the countries have rich mineral resources. Venezuela is a leading producer of oil, Colombia mines emeralds, gold and coal; silver, zinc, iron and tin have all been discovered in the mountainous areas of Bolivia and Peru. Agriculture varies from the subsistence farming practised by the Bolivian Indians on the high plateau around Lake Titicaca to the high levels of production of a country such as Ecuador, which is a leading exporter of bananas. Colombia, Bolivia and Peru are all suppliers of illegal drugs, particularly cocaine.

The people of these countries are descended from the native Indians and the European settlers who conquered the region in the sixteenth century. In Peru and Bolivia over half the people are of Indian blood, speaking the original Inca language, Quechua.

Lake Titicaca
Outside their reed-home on Lake Titicaca, these women are making clothes to be sold at market. Lake Titicaca lies between Peru and Bolivia and is the highest lake in the world.

Life in the Andes
In the south-west of Bolivia lies part of the high Andes mountain range. In this region the average yearly temperature is as low as four degrees Celsius. At these high altitudes no trees can survive, and it is too cold to grow crops. The Bolivian people who inhabit this area live by herding llamas, the hardy animals in the picture, which are kept for their wool and meat.

Lake Maracaibo, Venezuela

Oil being pumped up at a rig on Lake Maracaibo in north-west Venezuela. This is the country's largest oil-producing region and most of the oil comes from the lake itself. Originally foreign oil companies, especially from the USA, produced and marketed the oil. Then the Venezuelan government took control in order to keep all the profits for itself. Now one of the world's largest oil producers, Venezuela is numbered amongst South America's wealthier nations.

The Venezuelan government has to plan carefully for the future. It is exploring for new oil in order to keep the industry going for as long as possible, and at the same time is expanding the country's other industries, so that when the oil finally runs out, Venezuela will be able to support itself. Many of Venezuela's products are made from oil, for example petro-chemicals.

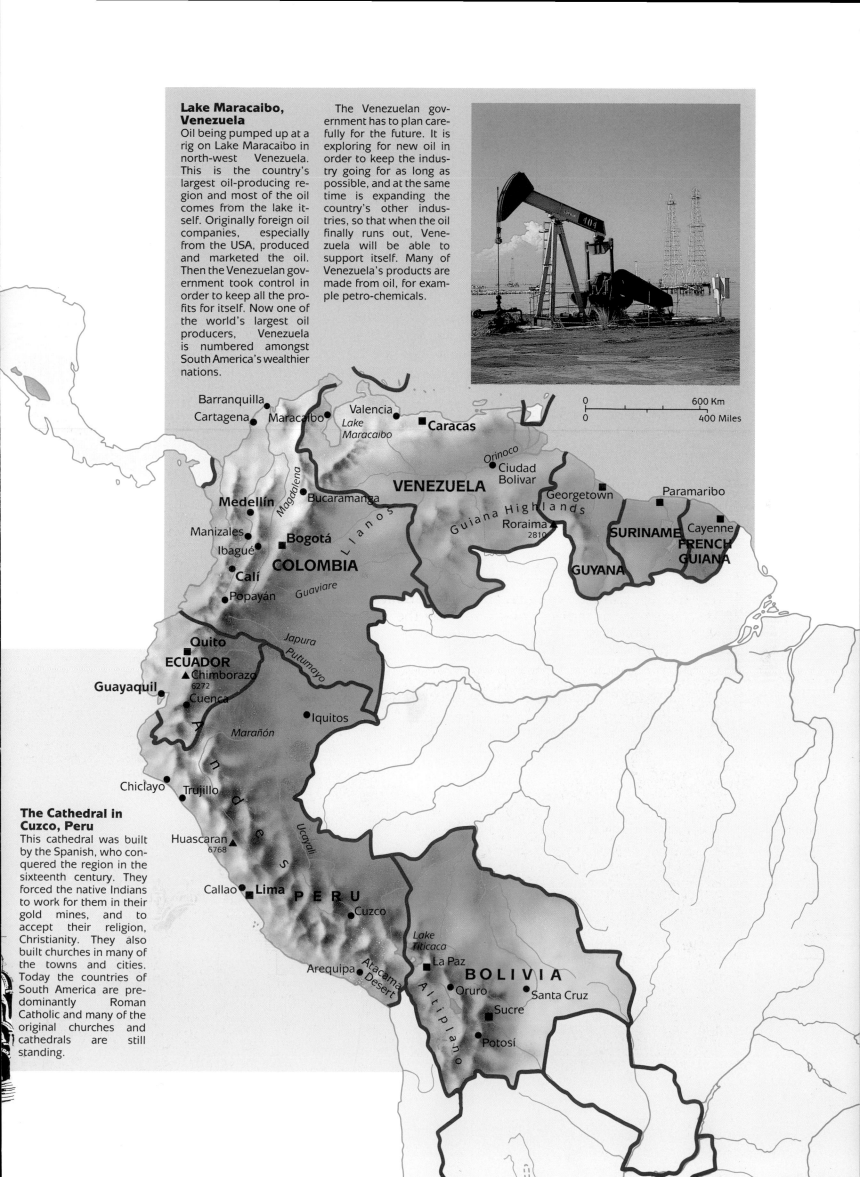

| 0 | | 600 Km |
| 0 | | 400 Miles |

Barranquilla
Cartagena Maracaibo
Valencia
Lake
Maracaibo
Caracas

Orinoco
Ciudad
Bolivar
VENEZUELA
Georgetown
Paramaribo
Medellín Bucaramanga
Guiana Highlands
Roraima▲
2810
SURINAME Cayenne
Manizales
Llanos
**FRENCH
GUIANA**
Ibagué **Bogotá**
COLOMBIA
GUYANA
Calí
Popayán
Guaviare

Quito
Japura
ECUADOR
Putumayo
▲Chimborazo
6272
Cuenca
Guayaquil
Iquitos
Marañón

Chiclayo
Trujillo
Ucayali

The Cathedral in Cuzco, Peru

This cathedral was built by the Spanish, who conquered the region in the sixteenth century. They forced the native Indians to work for them in their gold mines, and to accept their religion, Christianity. They also built churches in many of the towns and cities. Today the countries of South America are predominantly Roman Catholic and many of the original churches and cathedrals are still standing.

Huascaran▲
6768

Callao **Lima** **P E R U**
Cuzco
Lake
Titicaca
Arequipa La Paz **B O L I V I A**
Atacama
Desert
Oruro
Santa Cruz
Sucre
Altiplano
Potosí

BRAZIL

Brazil is the largest country in South America. For a long time it was governed by Portugal, and Portuguese is still the language spoken by most Brazilians. Brazil is a tropical country and it contains the largest area of tropical rainforest in the world.

The Amazon, the world's second longest river, runs through Brazil. For most of its course it flows through the hot, steamy jungles of the tropical rainforest. In north-east Brazil the climate is dry and farming is difficult, but further south there are vast grazing lands. Iron ore is mined in the south-east of the country, where coffee and oranges are also produced. These are important exports for Brazil. The main cities are situated in this region. São Paulo is one of South America's most crowded cities, but the beauty of Rio de Janeiro attracts visitors from all over the world. Brazil's capital is Brasilia, a new city that was built so that the government would be situated in the centre of the country.

Rainforest

Clearing away the rainforest in Brazil. Every year developers and timber companies destroy rainforest equal to three times the size of Switzerland. Unknown numbers of plants and animals are being lost, and soils washed away.

Rio de Janeiro

Rio's carnival is famous throughout the world. Every year during Mardi Gras thousands of people dress in spectacular costumes and parade through the streets. For days on end there is singing and dancing to the rhythms of Brazilian music.

Brazil's cities

Many people in Brazil's cities live in very poor conditions. Some live in old houses which are ready to collapse.

0	600 Km
0	400 Miles

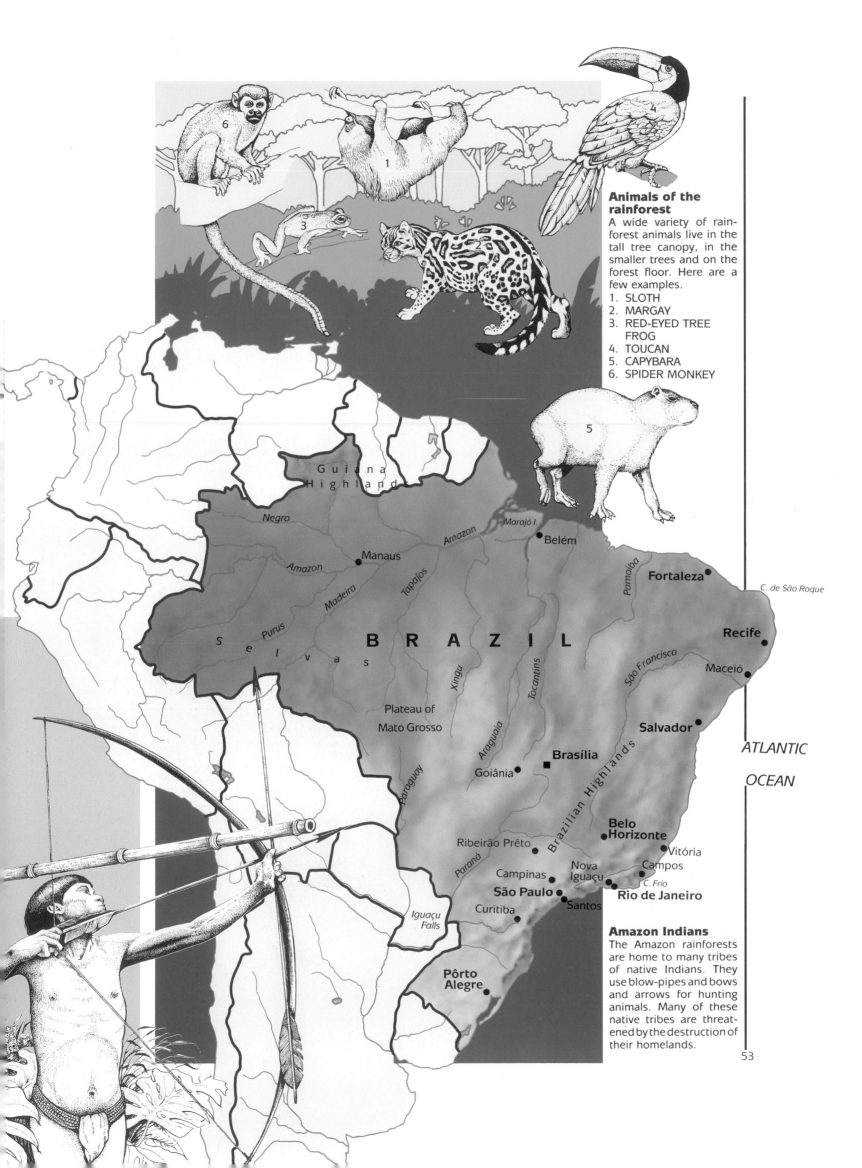

Animals of the rainforest

A wide variety of rainforest animals live in the tall tree canopy, in the smaller trees and on the forest floor. Here are a few examples.

1. SLOTH
2. MARGAY
3. RED-EYED TREE FROG
4. TOUCAN
5. CAPYBARA
6. SPIDER MONKEY

Guiana Highlands

Negro

Amazon

Manaus

Marajó I.

Belém

Madeira

Tapajós

Purus

Selvas

Parnaíba

Fortaleza

C. de São Roque

B R A Z I L

Recife

Maceió

São Francisco

Xingu

Tocantins

Plateau of Mato Grosso

Araguaia

Salvador

Paraguay

Brasília

Goiânia

Brazilian Highlands

Belo Horizonte

Paraná

Ribeirão Prêto

Vitória

Nova Iguaçu

Campos

Campinas

C. Frio

São Paulo

Rio de Janeiro

Curitiba

Santos

Iguaçu Falls

ATLANTIC

OCEAN

Pôrto Alegre

Amazon Indians

The Amazon rainforests are home to many tribes of native Indians. They use blow-pipes and bows and arrows for hunting animals. Many of these native tribes are threatened by the destruction of their homelands.

53

SOUTHERN SOUTH AMERICA

Like much of the continent, many parts of southern South America were conquered by the Spanish in the sixteenth century. Since then immigrants from many European countries have settled there. Some areas, such as the sub-tropical forests of Paraguay, and the Andes Mountains of Chile, still have Indian inhabitants.

Most people live in the large cities: Buenos Aires, the capital of Argentina, is home to one-third of Argentina's population, while one-half of the people in Uruguay live in its capital, Montevideo. On the vast areas of grassland in Paraguay, Uruguay and Argentina sheep and cattle are grazed, supplying the meat-packing, wool and textile industries. Argentina also produces wheat and maize, grown on fields in the Pampas region. In Patagonia, in the south, there are big reserves of oil and gas. Chile has huge mineral deposits, and is one of the world's largest suppliers of copper, which is found in the Atacama Desert in the northern part of the country.

Gauchos
Gauchos are similar to North American cowboys. Traditionally their main job was to take cattle to the markets in the large towns of Argentina, Paraguay and Uruguay, often riding for several weeks through the grasslands. Today, many of them ride motorbikes and tractors instead of horses.

Chiloé island
The large island of Chiloé lies close to the mainland near Puerto Montt in Chile. The climate is wet and the area prone to earthquakes. The island's ancient port, Castro, was founded in 1567. Many of the houses there are built on stilts in order to raise them clear of soft ground and the flood-water from tidal waves.

Football crazy
Football is the national sport of all the Latin American countries. Uruguay and Argentina have both won the World Cup twice.

The Chilean landscape

Chile, the longest, narrowest country on Earth, is no more than 380 kilometres wide at any point, but is 4265 kilometres long, stretching down South America's west coast between the Andes mountains and the Pacific Ocean.

The south of this country is a landscape of lakes, roaring waterfalls and fuming volcanoes capped with snow, as can be seen in this view of Lake Villarrica. Around Cape Horn, the southernmost tip of South America, lie many thousands of islands and a labyrinth of fjords.

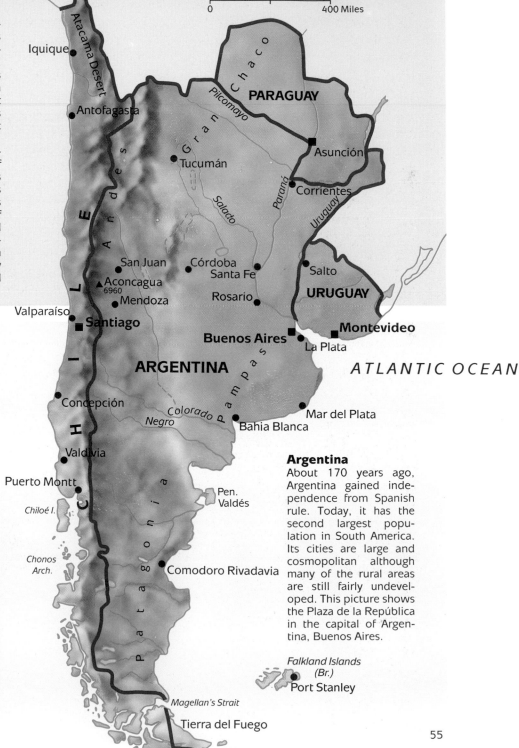

0 | 600 Km
0 | 400 Miles

Iquique

Atacama Desert

Gran Chaco

PARAGUAY

Pilcomayo

Antofagasta

Asunción

Tucumán

Salado

Paraná

Corrientes

Uruguay

Andes

San Juan

Córdoba

Santa Fe

Salto

▲ Aconcagua
6960

Mendoza

Rosario

URUGUAY

Valparaíso

■ **Santiago**

Buenos Aires ■

La Plata

Montevideo

CHILE

ARGENTINA

Pampas

ATLANTIC OCEAN

Concepción

Colorado

Mar del Plata

Negro

Bahia Blanca

Valdivia

Argentina

About 170 years ago, Argentina gained independence from Spanish rule. Today, it has the second largest population in South America. Its cities are large and cosmopolitan although many of the rural areas are still fairly undeveloped. This picture shows the Plaza de la República in the capital of Argentina, Buenos Aires.

Puerto Montt

Chiloé I.

Pen. Valdés

Patagonia

Chonos Arch.

Comodoro Rivadavia

Falkland Islands (Br.)

Port Stanley

Magellan's Strait

Tierra del Fuego

55

C. Horn

ASIA

Asia is the largest of the continents and contains the two most populous countries in the world: China and India. In contrast, many of the 14,000 islands that make up Indonesia are sparsely populated or uninhabited.

The variety of landscape is huge. In northern Russia lies a vast area of *taiga* (coniferous forest), while the desert lands of the Gobi cover much of Mongolia. Farther south lie China's vast cultivated plains, and on the edge of the Pacific Ocean volcanic islands support lush tropical vegetation.

North of the Indian subcontinent, in Nepal and Tibet, the Himalayas and the high Tibetan Plateau form the 'rooftop of the world'. From these icy heights flow the tributaries of some of the great river systems of this region, the Yangtze, Irrawaddy, Mekong, Ganges and Indus rivers. cont. page 58

A high mountain peak in the Himalayas in Nepal.

Asia
Highest point Mount Everest (Nepal/China) 8848m. (29,028ft.)
Lowest point Shore of Dead Sea (Israel/Jordan) 399m. (1310ft.) below sea level
Longest river Yangtze (China) 6300km. (3915mi.)
Largest lake Caspian Sea (Asia) 372,000sq.km. (143,630sq.mi.)

INDIA
Official name Bharat
Area 3,287,590 sq. km. (1,269,350 sq. miles)
Population 766,135,000
Capital New Delhi (pop. 6,220,000)
Largest cities Calcutta (9,166,000) Bombay (8,202,000) Madras (4,277,000) Bangalore (2,914,000)
Currency Indian Rupee
Official language(s) Hindi and English (14 regional languages are also spoken)
Chief products Rice, wheat, sugar cane, jute, cotton, tea, coal, chemicals, fertilizers, vehicles
Exports Textiles, jewellery, clothing, leather goods, iron ore, tea, fish
Imports Crude oil, iron and steel, precious stones

MALDIVES
Area 298 sq. km. (115 sq. miles)
Population 189,400
Capital Malé

CHINA (PEOPLE'S REPUBLIC OF CHINA)
Official name Zhonghua Renmin Gonghe-guo
Area 9,571,300 sq. km. (3,695,500 sq. miles)
Population 1,072,330,000
Capital Beijing (Peking) (pop. 5,970,000)
Currency Yuan
Official language(s) Mandarin (also Cantonese and other dialects)
Chief products Coal, iron, steel, machinery, textiles, chemicals, oil, tin, minerals, rice, tea, silkworms, pulses
Exports Livestock, textiles, ore, metals, tea, clothing
Imports Vehicles, machinery, chemicals

HONG KONG (UK)
Area 1067 sq. km. (412 sq. mi.)
Population 5,533,000
MACAO (PORTUGAL)
Area 16 sq, km. (6 sq. mi.)
Population 392,000

JAPAN
Official name Nihon
Area 377,815 sq. km. (145,875 sq. miles)
Population 123,600,000
Capital Tokyo (pop. 8,155,781)
Currency Yen
Official language(s) Japanese
Chief products Vehicles, machinery, electrical goods, iron, steel, chemicals, textiles, fish, rice
Exports Steel, vehicles, electrical equipment, ships
Imports Minerals, crude oil, raw materials, food

SRI LANKA
Area 64,453 sq. km. (24,886 sq. miles)
Population 17,200,000
Capital Colombo
Chief products Graphite, minerals, precious stones

INDONESIA
Area 1,904,569 sq. km. (735,358 sq. miles)
Population 170,534,000
Capital Jakarta
Official language(s) Bahasa and Indonesian
Chief products Copra, spices, palm oil, sugar, rubber, tea, coffee, tobacco, rice, oil, timber, minerals

BHUTAN
Area 47,000 sq. km. (18,147 sq. miles)
Population 1,447,000
Capital Thimphu

BRUNEI
Area 5765 sq. km. (2226 sq. miles)
Population 226,000
Capital Bandar Seri Begawan

PAKISTAN
Official name Islami Jamhuriya-e-Pakistan
Area 803,943 sq. km. (310,403 sq. miles)
Population 102,238,000
Capital Islamabad
Official language(s) Urdu
Chief products Cotton, rice, wheat, sugar cane, maize, tobacco, salt, leather, wool, fertilizers, paints, carpets, paper

SINGAPORE
Area 616 sq. km. (238 sq. miles)
Population 2,647,100
Chief products Oil refining, chemicals, ships, electrical equipment, paper, machinery, textiles

NEPAL
Area 147,181 sq. km. (56,827 sq. miles)
Population 17,632,960
Capital Kathmandu
Chief products Cattle, corn, rice, oil seeds, wheat

MONGOLIA
Area 1,565,000 sq. km. (604,250 sq. miles)
Population 1,900,000
Capital Ulan Bator
Chief products Livestock, wool, hides and skins, minerals

NORTH KOREA
Area 120,538 sq. km. (7929 sq. miles)
Population 21,390,000
Capital Pyongyang
Chief products Chemicals, iron and steel, rice, corn, machinery, wheat

SOUTH KOREA
Area 99,222 sq. km. (38,310 sq. miles)
Population 42,082,128
Capital Seoul
Chief products Chemicals, textiles, iron and steel, rice, electrical equipment

BANGLADESH
Area 143,998 sq. km. (55,598 sq. miles)
Population 102,563,000
Capital Dhaka
Chief products Jute, paper, textiles, natural gas, leather, rice, sugar cane

MYANMAR (BURMA)
Area 672,552 sq. km. (261,218 sq. miles)
Population 39,411,000
Capital Rangoon
Chief products Silk, tin, timber, copper, rubber

THAILAND
Area 513,115 sq. km. (198,115 sq. miles)
Population 54,536,000
Capital Bangkok
Chief products Teak, bamboo, fish, tin, iron ore, natural gas, rice, rubber

LAOS
Area 236,800 sq. km. (91,400 sq. miles)
Population 4,218,000
Capital Vientiane
Chief products Cattle, citrus fruits, coffee, opium, cotton, teak, rice, salt

KAZAKHSTAN
Area 2,717,300 sq. km. (1,049,155 sq. miles)
Population 16,690,300
Capital Alma-Ata
Chief products Grain, cotton, fruit, coal, petroleum, electric power

CAMBODIA
Area 181,035 sq. km. (69,898 sq. miles)
Population 7,688,000
Capital Phnom Penh
Chief products Cement, paper, textiles, cattle, rice

KYRGYZSTAN
Area 198,500 sq. km. (76,640 sq. miles)
Population 4,372,000
Capital Bishkek
Chief products Grain, vegetables, coal, petroleum, cement, steel

VIETNAM
Area 328,566 sq. km. (127,246 sq. miles)
Population 62,808,000
Capital Hanoi
Chief products Cement, iron and steel, paper, coal, textiles, rice

TAJIKISTAN
Area 143,100 sq. km. (55,250 sq. miles)
Population 5,112,000
Capital Dushanbe
Chief products Cotton, vegetables, grain, coal, petroleum, natural gas

PHILIPPINES
Area 300,000 sq. km. (115,831 sq. miles)
Population 56,004,000
Capital Manila
Chief products Fish, pineapples, rice, metals, oil products, mother of pearl, mahogany, textiles

UZBEKISTAN
Area 447,400 sq. km. (172,740 sq. miles)
Population 20,322,000
Capital Tashkent
Chief products Cotton, vegetables, grain, paper products, plastics

See page 35 for information on other former Soviet republics.

BHUTAN

BRUNEI

MALDIVES

TAIWAN
Area 35,590 sq. km. (13,890 sq. miles)
Population 19,258,053
Capital Taipei

MALAYSIA
Area 329,758 sq. km. (127,320 sq. miles)
Population 16,921,000
Capital Kuala Lumpur
Chief products Rubber, rice, cacao, coconuts, minerals, palm oil, pepper

TURKMENISTAN
Area 488,100 sq. km. (188,455 sq. miles)
Population 3,621,700
Capital Ashkhabad
Chief products Cotton, vegetables, grain, petroleum, fertilizers

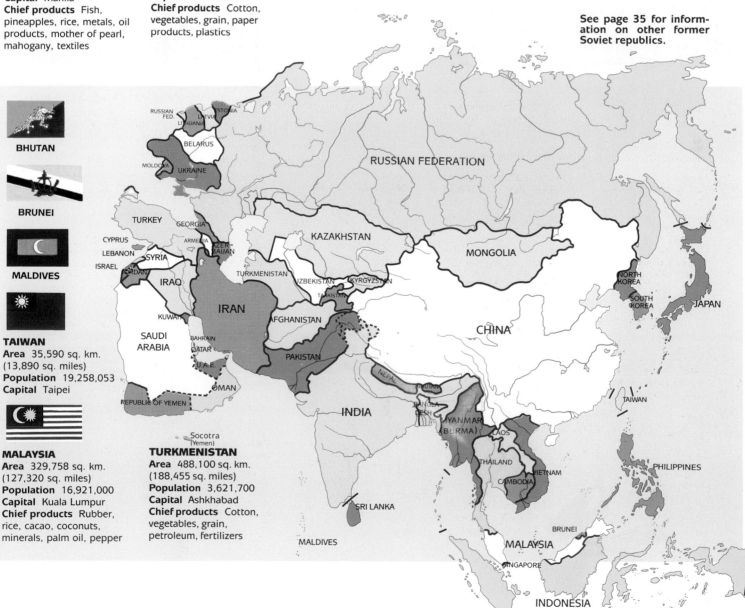

The Middle East is the name given to that part of south-west Asia which lies between the Mediterranean and the Indian subcontinent. Its geographical position has led to a mix of peoples and cultures from both East and West. A series of mountain ranges runs across the north of the region from the Taurus Mountains in Turkey to the Hindu Kush, the western foothills of the Himalayas, in Afghanistan.

The climate along the Mediterranean coast is temperate but farther south the Arabian peninsula and central Iran are sparsely-populated, desert lands. The 'empty quarter' in Saudi Arabia is uninhabited except for a small number of nomadic Bedouin. Most of the population lives in the coastal regions next to the Red Sea, the Gulf and the Indian Ocean. Oil exploitation, shipping and some agriculture enable coastal communities to thrive.

Sunset over Jerusalem city with the Dome of the Rock in the background.
(top) Nomadic huts or *yurts* in the Hindu Kush region of Afghanistan.

IRAN
Official name Jomhori-e-Islami-e-Irân
Area 1,648,00 sq. km. (636,296 sq. miles)
Population 49,857,384
Capital Tehran (pop. 6,022,029)
Largest cities Mashhad (1,500,000)
Esfahan (1,000,000)
Tabriz (852,296)
Shiraz (800,416)
Bakhtaran (531,350)
Currency Iranian Rial
Official language(s) Farsi (Persian) (Turkish, Kurdish and Arabic are also spoken)
Chief products Oil, natural gas, iron ore, coal, zinc and lead, sugar, textiles, cement, wheat, rice, sugar beet, tobacco, fish, cotton, steel, oil seeds, wool
Exports Oil, gas, carpets, fruit, caviar, textiles, cement
Imports Livestock, minerals, chemicals, iron and steel, machinery, vehicles

ISRAEL
Official name Medinat Israel
Area 21,946 sq. km. (8473 sq. miles)
Population 4,406,500
Capital Jerusalem (pop. 428,668)
Largest cities Tel-Aviv - Yafo (327,625)
Haifa (235,775)
Currency New Shekel
Official language(s) Hebrew (Arabic is also spoken)
Chief products Citrus fruits (especially oranges), olives, rice, vegetables, tobacco, wheat, barley, corn, sesame, chemicals, clothing, finished diamonds, machinery, salts, phosphates
Exports Citrus fruits (oranges), vegetables, finished diamonds, pearls, manufactured goods
Imports Rough diamonds, electrical equipment, iron and steel, chemicals, crude oil, cereals, vehicles

SAUDI ARABIA
Official name Al-Mamlaka al-Arabiya as-Sa'udiya
Area 2,400,900 sq. km. (926,745 sq. miles)
Population 13,612,000
Capital Riyadh (pop. 666,840)
Largest cities Jiddah (Administrative capital) (561,104)
Mecca (366,801)
Ta'if (204,857)
Medina (198,186)
Dammam (127,844)
Hofuf (101,271)
Currency Saudi Riyal
Official language(s) Arabic
Chief products Oil, cement, fertilizers, steel, petro-chemicals, camels, citrus fruits, dates, goats, rice, vegetables, wheat
Exports Crude and refined oil
Imports Food, tobacco, metals and metal products, precision tools, precious stones and metals, ceramics, glass

TURKEY
Official name Türkiye Cumhuriyeti
Area 779,452 sq. km. (300,948 sq. miles)
Population 50,664,458
Capital Ankara (pop. 2,235,035)
Largest cities Istanbul (5,475,982)
Izmir (1,489,772)
Adana (777,554)
Bursa (612,510)
Currency Turkish Lira
Official language(s) Turkish (Kurdish is also spoken)
Chief products Iron and steel, fertilizers, machinery, vehicles, processed food and drink, paper products, textiles, barley, corn, cotton, fruit, wheat
Exports Agricultural products, textiles, tobacco, citrus fruits, figs, olives, salt, hazelnuts
Imports Machinery, iron and steel, petroleum, medicines, dyes, vehicles

SYRIA
Official name Al-Jumhuriya al-Arabiya as-Souriya
Area 185,180 sq. km. (71,498 sq. miles)
Population 10,612,000
Capital Damascus
Official language(s) Arabic
Chief products Oil, natural gas, phosphates, asphalt, iron ore, tobacco, petroleum products, cotton

LEBANON
Official name Al-Jumhuriya al-Lubnaniya
Area 10,452 sq. km. (4036 sq. miles)
Population 2,762,000
Capital Beirut
Official language(s) Arabic (French is also spoken)
Chief products Cement, chemicals, electrical equipment, furniture, textiles, citrus fruits

JORDAN
Official name Al-Mamlaka al-Urduniya al-Hashemiyah
Area 97,740 sq. km. (37,738 sq. miles)
Population 3,804,000
Capital Amman
Official language(s) Arabic
Chief products Barley, fruit, olives, goats, lentils, sheep, vegetables, wheat, phosphates

IRAQ
Official name Al-Jumhuriya al-'Iraqiya
Area 438,317 sq. km. (169,235 sq. miles)
Population 16,110,000
Capital Baghdad
Official language(s) Arabic (Kurdish is also spoken)
Chief products Oil, dates, fruit, wheat, barley, rice, millet, cotton, tobacco, livestock, leather products

AFGHANISTAN
Official name Da Jamhuriat Afghanistan
Area 652,225 sq. km. (251,773 sq. miles)
Population 18,614,000
Capital Kabul
Official language(s) Pashtu, Dari
Chief products Cement, textiles, rugs, coal, gold, natural gas, corn, cotton, nuts, rice, sheep

KUWAIT
Official name Dawlat al-Kuwayt
Area 17,818 sq. km. (6880 sq. miles)
Population 1,872,569
Capital Kuwait
Official language(s) Arabic
Chief products Oil, natural gas, fruit, vegetables, fish (especially shrimps)

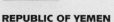

REPUBLIC OF YEMEN
Official name Al-Jumhuriya al-Yemeniya
Area 477,530 sq. km. (184,345 sq.miles)
Population 11,494,353
Capital San'a
Official language(s) Arabic
Chief products Sorghum, sesame, dyes, fish, refined oil, coffee, khat, fruit, barley, cotton, dates, vegetables

OMAN
Official name Saltanat Uman
Area 271,950 sq. km. (104,970 sq. miles)
Population 1,334,000 (estimate)
Capital Muscat
Official language(s) Arabic (English is also spoken)
Chief products Oil, coconuts, dates, limes, livestock, sugar cane

UNITED ARAB EMIRATES
Official name Al-Imarat al-Arabiya al-Muttahida
Area 75,150 sq. km. (29,010 sq. miles)
Population 11,384,000
Capital Abu Dhabi
Official language(s) Arabic
Chief products Oil, fish (especially shrimps), dates

QATAR
Official name Dawlat Qatar
Area 11,437 sq. km. (4416 sq. miles)
Population 369,079
Capital Doha
Official language(s) Arabic (English is also spoken)
Chief products Oil and petroleum products

BAHRAIN
Official name Dawlat al-Bahrayn
Area 691.2 sq. km. (266.9 sq. miles)
Population 412,000
Capital Manama
Official language(s) Arabic (English is also spoken)
Chief products Oil, aluminium, boats, building materials, petroleum products, plastics, grains

TURKEY AND NEAR EAST

Turkey and the Near East (which includes the countries of Syria, Jordan, Lebanon and Israel) lie at the eastern end of the Mediterranean and extend south to the deserts of Saudi Arabia. People of three main religions – Islam, Judaism and Christianity – inhabit this region and all regard Jerusalem as their holy city. Religious differences are the cause of much conflict in the Near East. In 1948, Israel was created as a land for Jews in part of the traditionally Muslim country of Palestine. The dispossessed Palestinians have been fighting to regain their territory ever since.

Much of Turkey and the coastal regions of Syria, Lebanon and Israel have a warm Mediterranean climate. Here the staple foods of wheat and barley are grown, as well as export crops such as tobacco, cotton, hazelnuts, citrus fruits, figs and olives. Farther east the land is hot, dry desert where agriculture is impossible without irrigation. The Dead Sea, the lowest point on the Earth, is mined for its rich salt deposits.

The 'Cotton Castle'
Many tourists visit Turkey for its unspoilt beauty. These scenic chalk terraces lie inland, near Denizli. In Turkish their name is 'Pamukkale' which means 'Cotton Castle'. Tourists come here to bathe in the spring water, which comes out of the ground at temperatures of up to 35 degrees Celsius.

A cotton factory in Syria
Cotton is grown extensively on the cultivated steppe lands of northeast Syria, the major agricultural region around the Euphrates and Asi rivers. This textile factory in Damascus is one of many which produces material for export. Best known is the heavy, patterned fabric *damask* which takes its name from the city.

Israel — land of the Jews
At their prayers Jews wear *tephillin*, small boxes containing Hebrew scriptures reminding them to live by the Law of God.

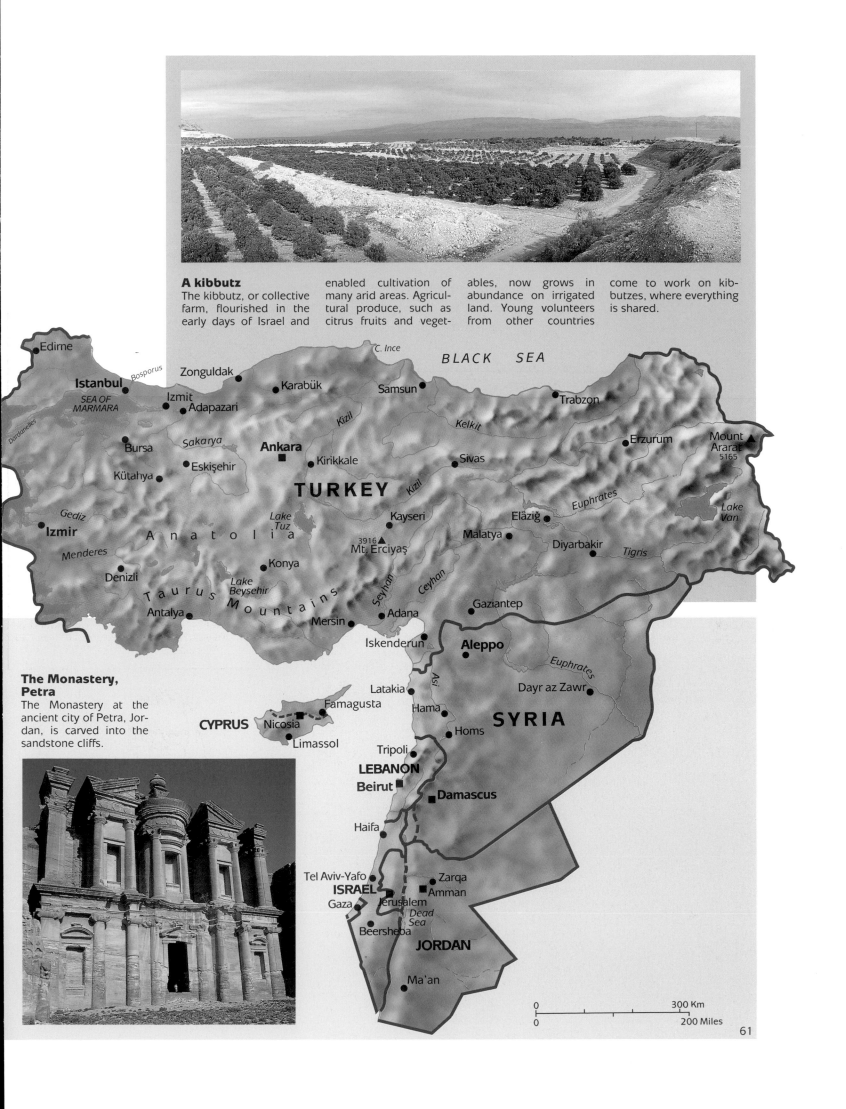

A kibbutz
The kibbutz, or collective farm, flourished in the early days of Israel and enabled cultivation of many arid areas. Agricultural produce, such as citrus fruits and vegetables, now grows in abundance on irrigated land. Young volunteers from other countries come to work on kibbutzes, where everything is shared.

The Monastery, Petra
The Monastery at the ancient city of Petra, Jordan, is carved into the sandstone cliffs.

BLACK SEA

Edirne

Bosporus

Istanbul
SEA OF MARMARA
Dardanelles

Zonguldak

Izmit
Adapazari

Karabük

C. Ince

Samsun

Trabzon

Kizil

Kelkit

Erzurum

Mount Ararat
5165

Bursa
Sakarya
Ankara
Eskişehir

Kirikkale

Sivas

Euphrates

Lake Van

Kütahya

Gediz

Izmir

A n a t o l i a

Lake Tuz

Kizil

Kayseri

Malatya

Elâziğ

Diyarbakir

Tigris

TURKEY

Menderes

3916▲
Mt. Erciyaş

Denizli

Konya

Lake Beyşehir

T a u r u s   M o u n t a i n s

Seyhan

Ceyhan

Gaziantep

Antalya

Mersin

Adana

Iskenderun

Aleppo

Euphrates

Latakia

Asi

Dayr az Zawr

Famagusta

CYPRUS
Nicosia
Limassol

Hama

Homs

SYRIA

Tripoli

LEBANON
Beirut

Damascus

Haifa

Tel Aviv-Yafo
ISRAEL
Gaza
Jerusalem
Dead Sea

Zarqa
Amman

Beersheba

JORDAN

Ma'an

| 0 | | 300 Km |
| 0 | | 200 Miles |

61

ARABIAN PENINSULA

In common with all the Middle Eastern countries except Israel, the Arabian peninsula nations are mostly Islamic. The holiest of the Muslim cities, Mecca, is in Saudi Arabia. The people of this region are Arabs and they all speak a common language: Arabic.

The Arabian peninsula is a hot, dry land which is very largely desert. The only large area with enough rain to grow crops is in the highlands of Yemen. Otherwise, some farming is possible in desert 'oases', and other small areas where underground water is used to irrigate crops. The date palm is a common sight in such areas.

All the countries of the Arabian peninsula, except Yemen, have discovered large reserves of oil in recent times. Oil is pumped from underground into ships which export it to Europe, North America, Asia and Africa. The money from selling oil has made these countries very rich. Many new roads and buildings have been constructed, and some Arabs no longer ride camels as before but drive bright new cars.

Arabian desert
Parts of the desert are covered by shifting sand dunes. Some of these areas are so large they are known as 'sand seas', or *ergs* in Arabic. The *erg* of *Rub'al Khali*, or Empty Quarter, in Saudi Arabia is about the size of England and Wales put together.

A market, Yemen
At a market, or *souk*, in a town in Yemen a man weighs home-made sugared cakes before selling them. These cakes are a favourite delicacy. In many of the markets of Yemen each street has its own speciality — hats, sandals, medicinal potions, herbs, cloth and pottery are all laid out and bartered for. Shoppers fill their turbans with the day's purchases.

Oil in the Arabian peninsula

The photograph above, shows a Saudi Arabian oil refinery. Oil is the most important 'natural resource' in the countries of the Arabian peninsula, especially those around the Gulf such as Kuwait, Saudi Arabia, Qatar and the United Arab Emirates. In some parts the oil is found beneath the sea, in other areas it is beneath the desert. Once it has been extracted, most of the oil has to be transported to other countries. Oil found in southern Oman, for example, is pumped through a pipeline 450 kilometres to the north coast where it is loaded onto ships. The countries that import oil use it to make petroleum, diesel, chemicals and plastics.

Saudi Arabia exports more oil than any other country in the world. Japan and the USA are its main customers. The money Saudi Arabia earns from oil is used to buy all sorts of machinery and manufactured goods, and many of these are bought from Japan and the USA. Much of the money is also spent on building things: new roads, houses, offices, airports and mosques (far left). Saudi Arabia also buys much of its food from abroad since the people cannot grow enough of their own in the harsh climate. Saudi Arabia does not import any alcohol or any foods with pork in them. This is because their religion does not allow Muslims to eat pork or drink alcohol.

Mosque

The photograph shows a mosque in Abu Dhabi, in the United Arab Emirates. The mosque is the Muslim place of worship. Like churches in Christian countries, mosques are often very fine buildings, some many hundreds of years old. The most important mosques have several domes and a minaret, or tower. It is from the minaret that the muezzin, a mosque official, will call worshippers to prayer five times a day. Most of the inhabitants of the Arabian countries are Muslims, followers of Islam. This religion teaches that there is one God, Allah, and that Mohammed was his prophet. The Koran is the sacred book of Islam.

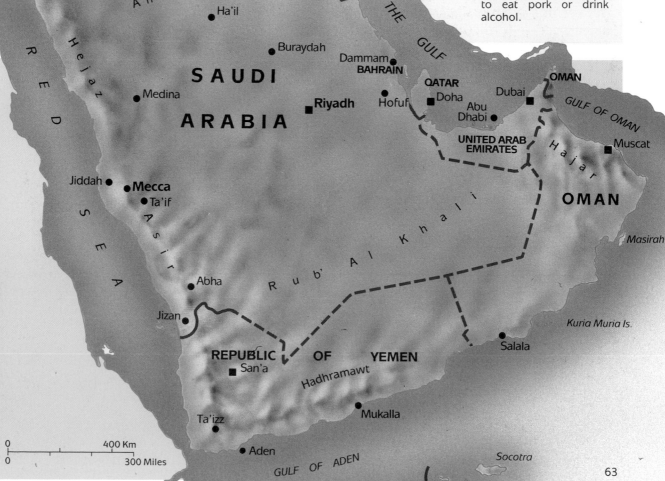

SOUTH-WEST ASIA

Between Mesopotamia and the Himalayas lie the countries of Iraq, Iran, and Afghanistan. Afghanistan is a poor country. Since 1979, civil war has ravaged the country. Many people are nomadic herders, constantly moving their animals to new grazing lands.

Iran and Iraq have become rich by exploiting their resources of oil and gas. Most of the oil is exported by tanker through the Persian Gulf, to Japan, the USA and Western Europe. Although Iran and Iraq are neighbours, religious differences and disputed territories led to war from 1980 to 1988. The Iraqis are Arabic, Sunni Muslims whereas the Iranians are descended from Asian peoples, speak Farsi, and are Shiite Muslims. Iraq invaded Kuwait in 1990, leading to the outbreak of war in January 1991. Allied forces from the US, Saudi Arabia, Britain, France and over twenty other nations defeated the Iraquis in February 1991.

Band-i-Amir Lake
Much of Afghanistan is desolate and bleak countryside which supports little or no vegetation. A high, inhospitable region called the Hindu Kush runs across the northeast of the country to meet the massive Hima-layan mountain range. Band-i-Amir lake (in the picture) is situated in an area known as Koh-i-Baba, north-west of Kabul. It is a natural reservoir, formed by the slow build-up of mineral deposits which have trapped the water. Irriga-tion ditches have been dug, and some members of the traditionally noma-dic Kuchi tribe have set-tled on land given by the government. Others move through these remote mountain areas in search of pastureland.

Persian carpets
The ancient tradition of carpet-making continues today in Iran. The carpets produced are better known as Persian rugs, and are prized as possessions world-wide. The rugs are worked by hand in silk or wool, using twine dyed in vivid colours and woven into intricate patterns. They are then washed and draped over rocks to dry in the sun.

The Marsh Arabs
The marshlands of southern central Iraq, around the Tigris and Euphrates rivers, are inhabited by the Marsh Arabs. The area is relatively inaccessible and as a result the Marsh Arabs' traditional way of life has remained almost untouched by outside influences. Many people still live in reed houses built on piles of rushes in up to two metres of water. Transport is by elegant canoes.

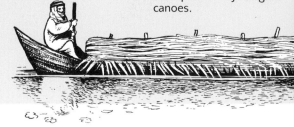

Persepolis, southern Iran

The ruins of the great palace of Persepolis as they stand today in southern Iran. Building work was started on the palace in 520BC under the order of Darius the First, ruler of the Persian Empire which covered much of modern Iran, Iraq, Afghanistan and the Near East. Darius and his court used Persepolis only once a year, at New Year, when tribute was brought to him by the various peoples of his vast Empire. Some of these tribute-bearers are depicted on the great staircase in the foreground of this picture.

Praying to Mecca

Every aspect of a Muslim's life is guided by the principles of Islam, and all Muslim men are required to pray five times each day. At the mosque every worshipper has his own mat on which he kneels, praying in the direction of Mecca, the birthplace of Muhammad.

Friday is the holy day for Muslims, work is forbidden and special prayers are conducted. The Koran, the holy book of Islam, records the preaching of Muhammad and lays down laws by which Muslims must live.

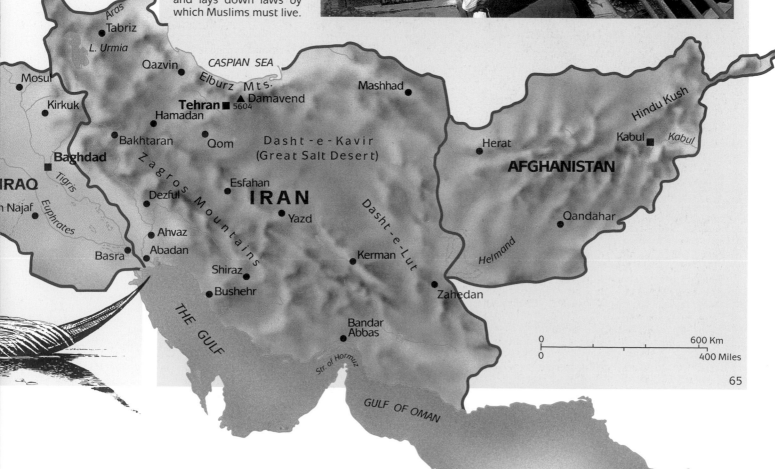

SOUTH ASIA

The region of South Asia is often called the Indian subcontinent. In the north, the high, snow-clad peaks and valleys of the Himalayas are sparsely populated. Farther south hot and overcrowded cities, such as Calcutta and Bombay, are home to millions of people, many of whom live on the streets or in temporary shanty towns.

Both India and Bangladesh have huge, and growing, populations — over 700 million people live in India alone. In the past people have settled here from all over Asia and more than 200 languages are still spoken across the region. Hinduism and Buddhism, two of the world's major religions, started in this area. Today, Pakistan and Bangladesh are mainly Muslim states and India is predominantly Hindu.

Rice, wheat and cotton are important crops and both India and Pakistan are major textile exporters. However, much agriculture is still subsistence farming, and relies on the annual monsoon rains which fall between June and October.

Quet

PAK

Baluchistan

Central Makran Ran

Karachi

Rice-growing in Pakistan
Rice is the main crop grown in the Punjab region of Pakistan. The rice-fields are flooded with water taken from the River Indus. Oxen are still used for the heavy labour.

The River Ganges at Varanasi
These Hindus are bathing in the River Ganges because the waters are believed to be holy. Every year millions of pilgrims come to the sacred Indian city of Varanasi to wash away their sins.

An Indian spice seller
This man is sitting at his spice stall in an Indian bazaar. Spices are very important in Indian food — one of the most popular dishes is highly-spiced curry. Some of the most common spices are pepper, ginger, mustard and cinnamon.

For centuries India has had a flourishing spice trade with countries in the West. Spices were important because, before refrigeration was invented, they were used to disguise the taste and smell of rotten food.

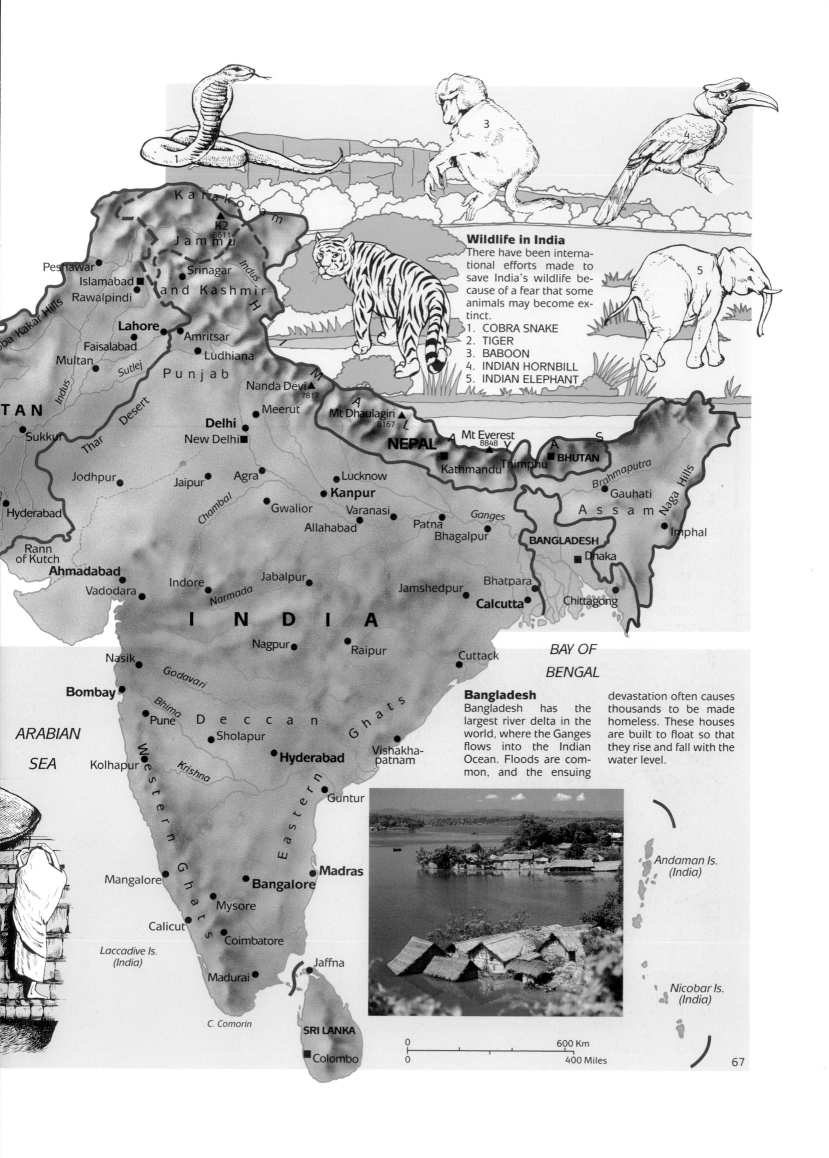

Wildlife in India

There have been international efforts made to save India's wildlife because of a fear that some animals may become extinct.

1. COBRA SNAKE
2. TIGER
3. BABOON
4. INDIAN HORNBILL
5. INDIAN ELEPHANT

Bangladesh

Bangladesh has the largest river delta in the world, where the Ganges flows into the Indian Ocean. Floods are common, and the ensuing devastation often causes thousands to be made homeless. These houses are built to float so that they rise and fall with the water level.

ARABIAN SEA

BAY OF BENGAL

K2
8611

Nanda Devi▲
7817

Mt Dhaulagiri ▲
8167

Mt Everest
8848

Peshawar
Islamabad
Rawalpindi
Lahore
Faisalabad
Multan
Sukkur
Hyderabad
Jodhpur
Jaipur
Agra
Delhi
New Delhi
Meerut
Srinagar
Amritsar
Ludhiana
Kathmandu
Thimphu
NEPAL
BHUTAN
Lucknow
Kanpur
Gwalior
Varanasi
Allahabad
Patna
Bhagalpur
Gauhati
Imphal
BANGLADESH
Dhaka
Ahmadabad
Vadodara
Indore
Jabalpur
Jamshedpur
Bhatpara
Calcutta
Chittagong
Nagpur
Raipur
Cuttack
Nasik
Bombay
Pune
Sholapur
Kolhapur
Hyderabad
Vishakhapatnam
Guntur
Mangalore
Bangalore
Madras
Mysore
Calicut
Coimbatore
Madurai
Jaffna
C. Comorin
SRI LANKA
Colombo

Karakoram
Jammu and Kashmir
Punjab
Thar Desert
Rann of Kutch
Indus
Sutlej
Chambal
Narmada
Ganges
Brahmaputra
Assam
Naga Hills
INDIA
Deccan
Godavari
Bhima
Krishna
Western Ghats
Eastern Ghats
Laccadive Is. (India)
Andaman Is. (India)
Nicobar Is. (India)

0   600 Km
0   400 Miles

SOUTH-EAST ASIA

The region known as south-east Asia includes more than 20,000 islands, mostly in Indonesia and the Philippines. Indonesia is the largest archipelago in the world, spanning 5120 kilometres — nearly the width of the USA.

The staple crop of the area is rice. Thailand, in particular, is known as the 'rice-bowl of Asia'. Other crops include coffee, rubber, sugar cane and coconuts. Most of the countries of this region have economies based on agriculture, and are relatively undeveloped. In contrast, Singapore is an international port and commercial centre, and Brunei, a tiny kingdom on the north coast of Borneo, is rich from oil. Indonesia, too, exports oil and has a lucrative and thriving tourist industry.

Mining in South-east Asia

A tin mine near Ipoh on the Malay Peninsula. Tin, which is mined throughout Malaysia, is a major source of income for the country.

Mining techniques are often basic, but modern technology is being introduced. From ports such as Port Kelang vast quantities of tin and Malaysia's other major commodity, rubber, are exported.

Teak logging

In Thailand's northern forests, domesticated elephants move felled teak trees to the saw mills. The elephants are used for their massive strength and mobility on ground which is unsuitable for heavy machinery.

Wildlife

Two exotic examples of the wildlife of the region are shown here.
1. PROBOSCIS MONKEY
2. MALAYAN TAPIR

Balinese dancers

These two young Balinese dancers are performing the graceful *legong* dance wearing flower headpieces and dazzling costumes. Such dances were originally performed to please the gods during festivals, when temples throughout the island were decorated with flowers and food offerings for them. Though they still play an important part in village life, many of the traditional rituals are now more often performed for the tourists who come to enjoy this tropical paradise.

The Shwesandaw Pagoda

The Shwesandaw Pagoda, the most highly revered religious building in Myanmar (Burma), is situated on the eastern bank of the River Irrawaddy, eight kilometres south of Pyè.

Buddhism is the main religion in this region. Every village has at least one monastery, and orange-clad monks are a common sight.

a Nang

ETNAM

i Minh City

SOUTH CHINA SEA

MALAYSIA

Bandar Seri Begawan
BRUNEI

▲ Kinabalu
4101
Sabah

Sarawak

Kuching   Borneo

Kapuas   Kalimantan   Mahakam

Barito

Banjarmasin

JAVA SEA   INDONESIA

Semarang
Yogyakarta   Madura
Surabaya
Malang   Bali

FLORES SEA
Lesser Sunda Islands
Sumbawa   Flores
Lombok

Sumba

Batan Is.

Babuyan Is.

Luzon

Quezon City

Manila

Mindoro

PHILIPPINES

Palawan   Panay   Samar

Cebu

Negros

SULU SEA   Mindanao   Davao

Sulu Arch.

CELEBES SEA

Manado   Halmahera

Sula Is.

Sulawesi (Celebes)   Buru   Moluccas

Ceram

Ujung Pandang   Butung   BANDA SEA

Wetar   Tanimbar Islands   Aru Is.

Alor

Timor

Maloke Range
▲ Puncak Jaya
5029

Irian Jaya

Jayapura

...ia, running
...Gobi Desert in
... east to the fertile

... size as the USA, yet its
...times as big, and it is one of
... world. Much of the population
...uth-east of the country, where rice
..., and silk is produced.

...eral reserves of coal, iron ore, oil and gas,
...west. Industry is developed around areas such
...g, China's capital, and in Shanghai where textiles
...ectrical goods are manufactured for export.

A Chinese canal scene

On the Great Plain in eastern China there are numerous canals which link up with some of the country's rivers. The canals bring water to dry districts and are used as transport routes. In this picture, two men are steering their barge with a cargo of hay through a town, the canal banks crowded with ramshackle houses.

The Potala Palace in Tibet

The Potala Palace stands on a high mount overlooking the city of Lhasa in the Himalayan mountains. It was once the residence of the Dalai Lama who is Tibet's spiritual leader, but in 1959 he was forced to leave the country by the Chinese Communists. Lhasa is a holy city for Tibetan Buddhists who worship the statue of Buddha in the temple of the Potala Palace.

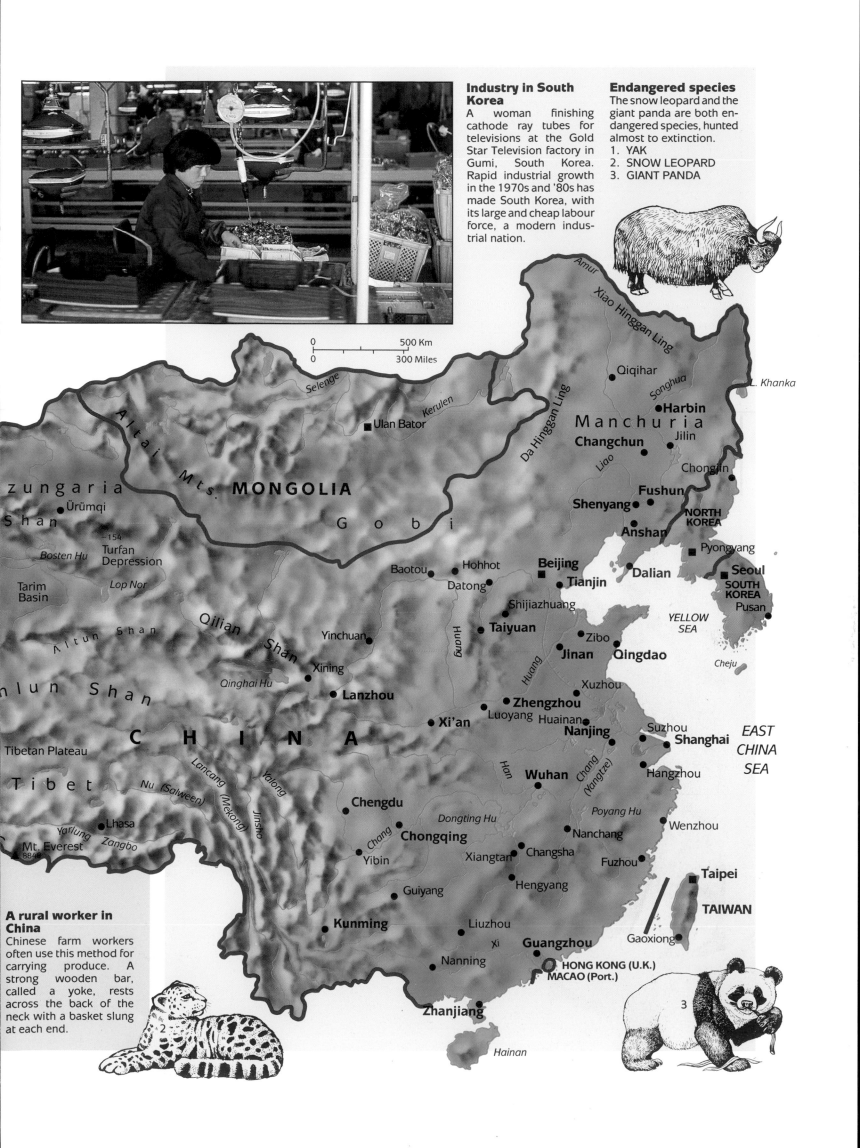

Industry in South Korea

A woman finishing cathode ray tubes for televisions at the Gold Star Television factory in Gumi, South Korea. Rapid industrial growth in the 1970s and '80s has made South Korea, with its large and cheap labour force, a modern industrial nation.

Endangered species

The snow leopard and the giant panda are both endangered species, hunted almost to extinction.
1. YAK
2. SNOW LEOPARD
3. GIANT PANDA

A rural worker in China

Chinese farm workers often use this method for carrying produce. A strong wooden bar, called a yoke, rests across the back of the neck with a basket slung at each end.

500 Km
300 Miles

Amur

Xiao Hinggan Ling

Qiqihar

L. Khanka

Songhua

Harbin

Manchuria

Da Hinggan Ling

Changchun

Jilin

Chongjin

Ulan Bator

Kerulen

Selenge

MONGOLIA

Gobi

Liao

Fushun

Shenyang

NORTH KOREA

Anshan

Pyongyang

Altai Mts.

Dzungaria

Ürümqi

Tian Shan

Baotou

Hohhot

Beijing

Tianjin

Dalian

Seoul

SOUTH KOREA

Pusan

Bosten Hu

Turfan Depression

−154

Datong

Shijiazhuang

Tarim Basin

Lop Nor

Qilian Shan

Yinchuan

Taiyuan

Zibo

Jinan

Qingdao

YELLOW SEA

Altun Shan

Xining

Huang

Cheju

Kunlun Shan

Qinghai Hu

Lanzhou

Xuzhou

Zhengzhou

Huang

Tibetan Plateau

C H I N A

Xi'an

Luoyang

Huainan

Nanjing

Suzhou

Shanghai

EAST CHINA SEA

Tibet

Lancang (Mekong)

Nu (Salween)

Yalong

Jinsha

Han

Wuhan

Chang (Yangtze)

Hangzhou

Lhasa

Yarlung Zangbo

Chengdu

Dongting Hu

Poyang Hu

Wenzhou

Mt. Everest
8848

Chang

Chongqing

Nanchang

Yibin

Xiangtan

Changsha

Fuzhou

Hengyang

Guiyang

Taipei

TAIWAN

Kunming

Liuzhou

Gaoxiong

Xi

Guangzhou

Nanning

HONG KONG (U.K.)
MACAO (Port.)

Zhanjiang

Hainan

JAPAN

Japan forms an archipelago in the Pacific comprising four main islands Honshu, Hokkaido, Shikoku and Kyushu, and over 3000 smaller, mostly uninhabited ones. This region is an earthquake zone and has over 50 active volcanoes. About seventy per cent of the country is mountainous and covered with forests, and most people live on the coastal plains.

The climate is sub-tropical in the south and colder in the north. On Hokkaido there is snow for up to four months in the winter. The warm-water Kuroshio Current brings to the south a rainy season in June and early July.

Japan is the world's most successful industrial nation, producing cars, motorcycles, electrical goods and half of the world's ships. All the raw materials to make these – such as iron ore, oil and coal – have to be imported as Japan has almost no natural resources. Japan is also one of the major fishing nations, catching large amounts of tuna, squid and octopus throughout the world for its home market.

A Japanese garden
The Japanese are famous for their garden design. In the past many European gardens were modelled on Japanese styles with pagodas, tea-houses, bridges and stone lanterns arranged around a pool or stream. Over the centuries growing trees has also developed into a sophisticated art in Japan, especially miniature trees like the bonsai which are grown in pots.

Karatsu Kunchi festival
The colourful Karatsu Kunchi festival takes place between 2 and 4 November. It is the autumn festival of the Karatsu Shrine. Fourteen impressive decorated floats are drawn through Karatsu city. Among other things, the floats depict a red lion, a turtle, Samurai helmets and a red sea bream, shown here in the photograph.

The Japanese at work

In large Japanese corporations today it is quite common for workers to participate in morning exercise routines on the factory floor. Many Japanese employees also wear a company uniform and take pride in their teamwork.

The people of Japan have become known world-wide as hard-working and efficient and are world leaders in the electronics field. Robots and advanced computers are used to produce the latest in household technology, such as microwave ovens, video cameras and recorders, and personal stereos.

SEA OF JAPAN

JAPAN

The tea ceremony

Conducting a tea ceremony. Although Japan is a modern westernized society, old traditions are carefully preserved. The tea ceremony is an ancient ritual that many Japanese women still continue to learn and practise. The bitter, green tea is served in delicate china and drunk slowly and reverently.

Harvesting rice

Farmers in this rice-field are gathering the rice into bundles to dry before threshing. Farming equipment is specially designed for Japanese farms, which are very small. Only fifteen per cent of the land in Japan is suitable for cultivation.

La Perouse Strait
C. Soya
Rebun
Rishiri
Wakkanai
Asahikawa
Hokkaido
Ishikari
Sapporo
Kushiro
Okushiri
C. Erimo
Hakodate
Tsugaru Str.
C. Shiriya
Aomori
Akita
Sendai
Sado
Niigata
Koriyama
C. Suzu
Iwaki
Shinano
Nagano
Utsunomiya
Kanazawa
Toyama
Maebashi
Tone
Honshu
Tokyo
Oki Is.
Gifu
Kawasaki
Yokohama
Chiba
L. Biwa
Mt. Fuji 3776
Yokosuka
Kyoto
Nagoya
Okayama
Himeji
Toyohashi
Shizuoka
Tsu Shima
Kobe
Hiroshima
Osaka
Hamamatsu
Shimonoseki
Kure
Sakai
Kitakyushu
Takamatsu
Wakayama
Matsuyama
Tokushima
Kochi
Fukuoka
C. Shio
Sasebo
Shikoku
Nagasaki
Oita
Kumamoto
Kyushu
Kagoshima
Osumi Is.
Tanega
Yaku
Amami
Tokuno
Ryukyu Islands
Okinawa

0 ——— 300 Km
0 ——— 200 Miles

AFRICA

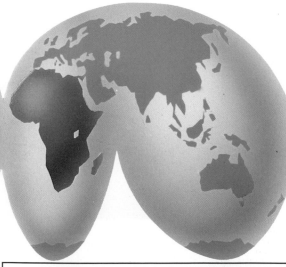

Africa is the second largest continent, stretching south from the Mediterranean Sea and lying between the Atlantic and the Indian Oceans. It is a land of infinite contrast. Much of northern Africa is covered by the Sahara, the biggest and hottest desert in the world, larger in size than the whole of Australia. In western and central regions, large areas of the coast are covered by dense tropical rainforests.

The Great Rift Valley runs from the Red Sea south to Malawi. East of the Rift are the mountain ranges of Ethiopia, Kenya and Tanzania, including the highest mountain peak in Africa at 5895 metres, Kilimanjaro. High plateaus in eastern and southern Africa are covered by rolling grasslands, known as savanna, home to much of Africa's abundant wildlife.

Open grassland, or *veldt*, in Drakensberg, on the border between South Africa and Lesotho.

Africa

Highest point Kilimanjaro (Tanzania) 5895m. (19,304ft.) above sea level
Lowest point Lake Assal (Djibouti) 155m. (509ft.) below sea level

Longest river Nile (Egypt) 6671km. (4145mi.)
Largest lake Victoria (Kenya/Uganda/Tanzania) 69,484 sq.km. (26,828 sq.mi.)

MOROCCO
Area 458,775 sq. km. (177,070 sq. miles)
Population 22,848,000
Capital Rabat
Chief products Clay, lead, marble, cement, food, soap, leather, textiles, almonds

GHANA
Area 238,537 sq. km. (92,100 sq. miles)
Population 13,704,000
Capital Accra
Chief products Textiles, bauxite, diamonds, gold, manganese, cacao, coffee

LIBYA
Area 1,775,500 sq. km. (685,524 sq. miles)
Population 3,624,000
Capital Tripoli
Chief products Oil, citrus fruits, dates, barley, olives, livestock, wheat

ALGERIA
Area 2,381,741 sq. km. (919,595 sq. miles)
Population 22,520,000
Capital Algiers
Chief products Iron ore, oil, phosphates, fruit, grain, vegetables, wine

NIGERIA
Area 923,768 sq. km. (356,669 sq. miles)
Population 101,992,000
Capital Lagos
Chief products Oil, tin, limestone, rubber, rice, chemicals, beans, cacao

EGYPT
Area 997,738 sq. km. (385,229 sq. miles)
Population 50,740,000
Capital Cairo
Chief products Iron ore, oil, manganese, salt, fish, cement, fertilizers, steel

ETHIOPIA
Area 1,251,282 sq. km. (483,123 sq. miles)
Population 46,184,000
Capital Addis Ababa
Chief products Barley, beans, coffee, cotton, hides and skins, livestock, timber

ZAIRE
Area 2,344,885 sq. km. (905,365 sq. miles)
Population 32,460,000
Capital Kinshasa
Chief products Cement, industrial diamonds, oil, coffee, cotton, copper, gold

IVORY COAST
Area 322,462 sq. km. (124,503 sq. miles)
Population 9,742,900
Capital Abidjan
Chief products Textiles, fruit, electrical equipment, ships, textiles, timber

CAMEROON
Area 475,442 sq. km. (183,569 sq. miles)
Population 10,822,000
Capital Yaoundé
Chief products Aluminium, oil, timber, natural rubber, bananas, cassava, cacao

SUDAN
Area 2,505,813 sq. km. (967,500 sq. miles)
Population 20,564,364
Capital Khartoum
Chief products Cotton, corn, dates, hides, skins, melons, peanuts, salt

KENYA
Area 580,367 sq. km. (224,081 sq. miles)
Population 21,163,000
Capital Nairobi
Chief products Coffee, corn, tea, sisal, sugar cane, cement, chemicals

UGANDA
Area 231,860 sq. km. (91,343 sq. miles)
Population 12,630,076
Capital Kampala
Chief products Copper, bananas, coffee, cotton, sweet potatoes, tea

NAME	AREA SQ. KM. (SQ. MILES)	POPULATION	CAPITAL
Angola	1,246,700 (481,354)	8,981,000	Luanda
Benin	112,622 (43,484)	4,304,000	Porto Novo
Botswana	582,000 (224,711)	1,169,000	Gaborone
Burkina	274,200 (105,870)	8,305,000	Ouagadougou
Burundi	27,834 (10,747)	5,001,000	Bujumbura
Central African Republic	622,984 (240,535)	2,740,000	Bangui
Chad	1,284,000 (495,800)	5,061,000	Ndjamena
Comoros	1862 (719)	484,000	Moroni
Congo	342,000 (132,047)	1,912,429	Brazzaville
Djibouti	23,200 (8958)	483,000	Djibouti
Equatorial Guinea	28,051 (10,830)	401,000	Malabo
Gabon	267,667 (103,347)	1,206,000	Libreville
The Gambia	11,295 (4361)	656,000	Banjul
Guinea	245,857 (94,926)	6,380,000	Conakry
Guinea-Bissau	36,125 (13,948)	906,000	Bissau
Lesotho	30,355 (11,720)	1,619,000	Maseru
Liberia	97,754 (37,743)	2,349,000	Monrovia
Madagascar	587,041 (226,658)	9,985,000	Antananarivo
Malawi	94,080 (36,315)	7,278,925	Lilongwe
Mali	1,240,190 (478,770)	8,206,000	Bamako
Mayotte (Fr)	373 (144)	50,400	Dzaoudzï
Mauritania	1,030,700 (397,950)	1,864,000	Nouakchott
Mauritius	2040 (788)	1,040,000	Port Louis
Namibia	824,292 (318,261)	1,595,000	Windhoek
Niger	1,267,000 (489,191)	7,249,000	Niamey
Réunion (Fr)	2512 (968.5)	574,800	Saint-Denis
Rwanda	26,338 (10,169)	6,710,000	Kigali
São Tomé and Príncipe	964 (372)	108,000	São Tomé
Senegal	196,722 (75,955)	6,397,000	Dakar
Seychelles	454 (175.3)	66,229	Victoria
Sierra Leone	71,740 (27,699)	3,849,000	Freetown
Somalia	637,657 (246,201)	4,760,000	Mogadishu
Swaziland	17,363 (6704)	676,000	Mbabane
Togo	56,785 (21,925)	3,052,000	Lomé
Tunisia	163,610 (63,170	7,464,900	Tunis
Western Sahara	266,000 (102,675)	160,000	El-Aaiún

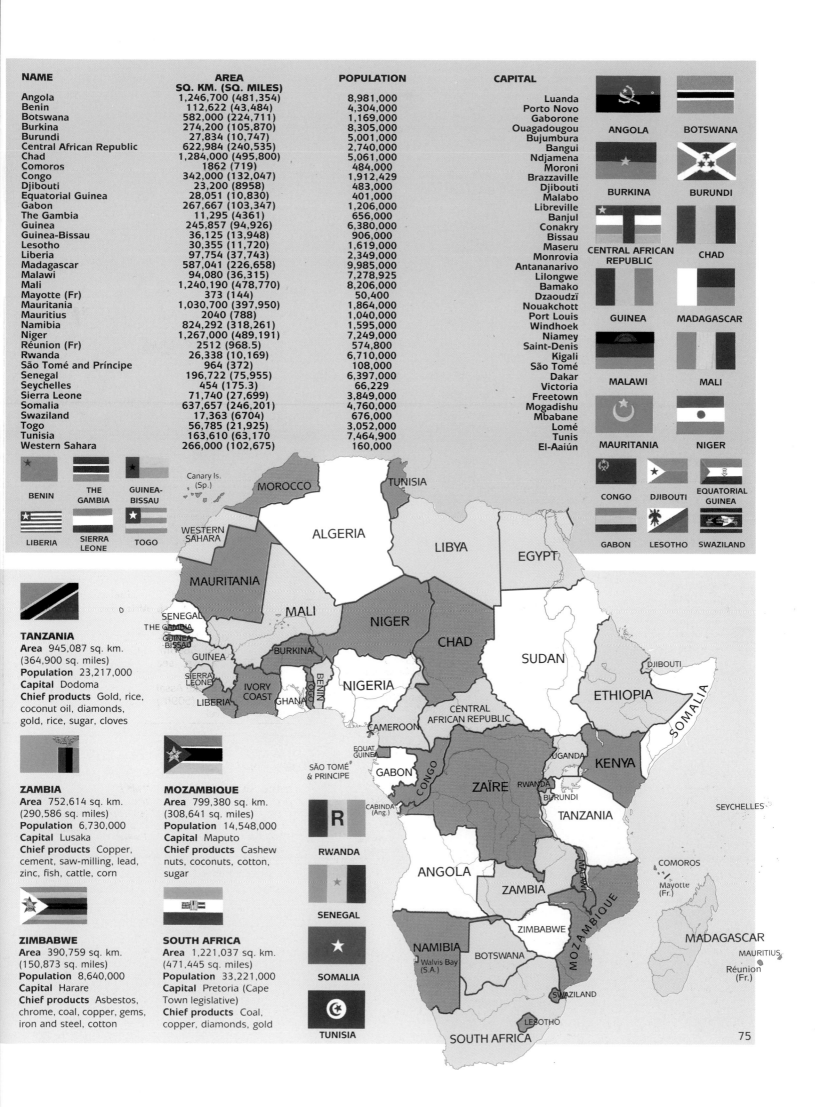

ANGOLA BOTSWANA BURKINA BURUNDI CENTRAL AFRICAN REPUBLIC CHAD GUINEA MADAGASCAR MALAWI MALI MAURITANIA NIGER CONGO DJIBOUTI EQUATORIAL GUINEA GABON LESOTHO SWAZILAND

BENIN THE GAMBIA GUINEA-BISSAU LIBERIA SIERRA LEONE TOGO

RWANDA SENEGAL SOMALIA TUNISIA

TANZANIA
Area 945,087 sq. km. (364,900 sq. miles)
Population 23,217,000
Capital Dodoma
Chief products Gold, rice, coconut oil, diamonds, gold, rice, sugar, cloves

ZAMBIA
Area 752,614 sq. km. (290,586 sq. miles)
Population 6,730,000
Capital Lusaka
Chief products Copper, cement, saw-milling, lead, zinc, fish, cattle, corn

MOZAMBIQUE
Area 799,380 sq. km. (308,641 sq. miles)
Population 14,548,000
Capital Maputo
Chief products Cashew nuts, coconuts, cotton, sugar

ZIMBABWE
Area 390,759 sq. km. (150,873 sq. miles)
Population 8,640,000
Capital Harare
Chief products Asbestos, chrome, coal, copper, gems, iron and steel, cotton

SOUTH AFRICA
Area 1,221,037 sq. km. (471,445 sq. miles)
Population 33,221,000
Capital Pretoria (Cape Town legislative)
Chief products Coal, copper, diamonds, gold

75

NORTHERN AFRICA

Ｎorth Africa is dominated by the Sahara, which stretches 4800 kilometres from the Atlantic coast in Mauritania across to the Red Sea in Sudan. It is the largest desert in the world; moreover, drought and destructive farming methods are causing it to expand southwards at the rate of about 10 kilometres a year. The climate along the Mediterranean coast enables crops such as dates and fruit to be grown, particularly in the foothills of the Atlas Mountains in the north-west. Huge irrigation systems are being developed by oil-rich Libya to pump water from deep beneath the desert to the fertile coastal areas 900 kilometres distant. However, farther south in Sudan and the highlands of Ethiopia, crop failures and drought have caused widespread famine.

Traditionally the Arab world has had a great influence on northern Africa, particularly in Egypt. The people of the region are mostly Muslim, and Arabic is widely spoken.

The River Nile
Much of Egypt is desert land which cannot support vegetation. The fertile regions on either side of the River Nile and in the Nile delta (seen here), form the major agricultural areas.

The River Nile is controlled by the Aswan Dam, completed in 1965, and now flows steadily all year, providing a constant supply of water for irrigation. Before the dam was built, the Nile regularly flooded its banks, washing nutrient-rich mud on to the land.

Madeira (Port.)

Ceuta (Sp.)Meli
Tangier (Sp
Rabat Fès
Casablanca
MOROCCO
Marrakesh

Canary Islands (Sp.)

El Aaiún

Dakhla **WESTERN SAHARA**

Fdérik

C. Blanc

A

S

MAURITANIA
Nouakchott

MALI
Tombouctou

Sénégal

Niger

Kayes

Bamako

The Dinka tribe
A Dinka man carrying a newly-born calf. The Dinka are a very tall, distinguished race from southern Sudan, a dry area where cultivation is limited. Most of the people are cattle herders, maintaining a traditional way of life.

Unlike the population

Ethiopia's famine

Ethiopia has been hit by severe drought for many years in succession. Lack of rain has meant that crops and livestock have perished, leaving many millions of people starving. There was a severe drought in 1973, but it was little publicized. In 1974 a Communist revolution overthrew Haile Selassie, who was emperor at that time, and since then drought and war have together caused widespread suffering. The wars being fought by the two provinces of Tigre and Eritrea in northern Ethiopia, in an attempt to win independence from Addis Ababan rule, have destroyed agriculture and made transport of food and medical supplies nearly impossible.

The devastating famine of 1985 was brought to the attention of the whole world, particularly by the pop music charity, Band Aid, which organized the Live Aid international music festival. The revenue from this en-

A Moroccan *souk*

All major towns in Morocco feature a bazaar, or *souk*, selling local and imported goods in noisy, colourful and pungent surroundings. Exotic items are sold including brassware, jewellery, spices and perfumes and fresh local produce is available too. Other activities include leather tanning and wool dying.

abled international aid agencies such as the Red Cross and Oxfam to provide medical supplies, food and shelter to many of the worst affected areas.

of the north, the people of southern Sudan, such as the Dinka and the Nuer, are not Muslim and do not speak Arabic. Conflict arising from these differences led to civil war in the 1980s. The spread of Islam and Arabic from the north continues to be a threat to the people of the south.

Algiers
Annaba
Tunis
Oran
Constantine
Sousse
ntains
Sfax
TUNISIA
Chott Djerid
Tripoli
Misratah
Benghazi
Alexandria
Port Said
Ghudamis
Qattara
Depression
▼−133
Cairo
Suez
Sinai
ERIA
L i b y a n
Asyut
EGYPT
L I B Y A
Marzuq
D e s e r t
A
R
A
Aswan
Nile
A h a g g a r H
▲Tahat
2918
Tamanrasset
L. Nasser
Tibesti
▲Emi Koussi
3415
RED
Nubian
Desert
Port
Sudan
Aïr.
N I G E R
Agades
C H A D
Atbara
Atbara
SEA
Er
Asmera
Omdurman
Kassala
itrea
Niamey
Zinder
L. Chad
Abéché
D a r f u r
El Obeid
Khartoum
White Nile
Blue Nile
Gonder
Danakil
L. Tana
DJIBOUTI
Djibouti
Ras
Asir
Ndjamena
Berbera
Hargeisa
Chari
S U D A N
Addis
Ababa■
Dire
Dawa
O g a d e n
Sarh
S u d d
Jima
ETHIOPIA
Shebele
S O M A L I A
Juba
Juba
Mogadishu

0
1200 Km
0
800 Miles

WESTERN, CENTRAL AND EASTERN AFRICA

In western Africa the Gulf of Guinea is bordered by many relatively small countries. Agriculture is developed, and crops such as cocoa, palm oil and groundnuts and hardwood trees are grown for export. Nigeria, the most populous country in Africa, has benefited from the discovery of large oil reserves in the late 1950s. Oil revenues have been used to finance new industries such as petro-chemical production, steel making and vehicle manufacture.

Dense tropical rainforests lie across central Africa, through which flows the River Zaïre. Like much of Africa, the countries of this region are made up of peoples of many different tribes – in Zaïre, for example, over 250 different local languages are spoken. To the east of the Great Rift Valley the flat grasslands of Tanzania and Kenya are sparsely populated by the Masai and other cattle herders. The climate in this region is particularly suited to growing coffee and tea, which are major exports.

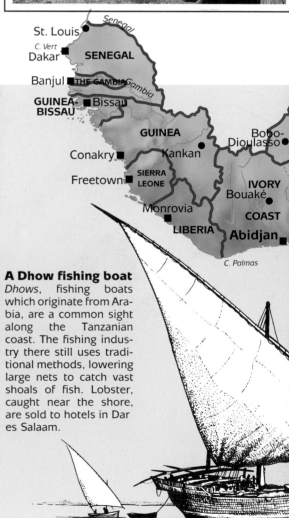

Lagos, Nigeria

Nigeria has a population of over 110 million, the largest in Africa, made up of 250 different groups and tribes including the Hausa, Yoruba and Ibo peoples. Lagos, the capital, is a thriving port on the south-west coast. The heart of the city, Lagos island, contains the administrative sector and is linked to the mainland and other islands by road bridges.

Huge oil reserves, discovered in the 1950s, have enabled Nigeria to build roads and ports and set up new industries. Despite this industrial development, Nigeria is still unable to produce enough food for its rapidly increasing population.

A Dhow fishing boat

Dhows, fishing boats which originate from Arabia, are a common sight along the Tanzanian coast. The fishing industry there still uses traditional methods, lowering large nets to catch vast shoals of fish. Lobster, caught near the shore, are sold to hotels in Dar es Salaam.

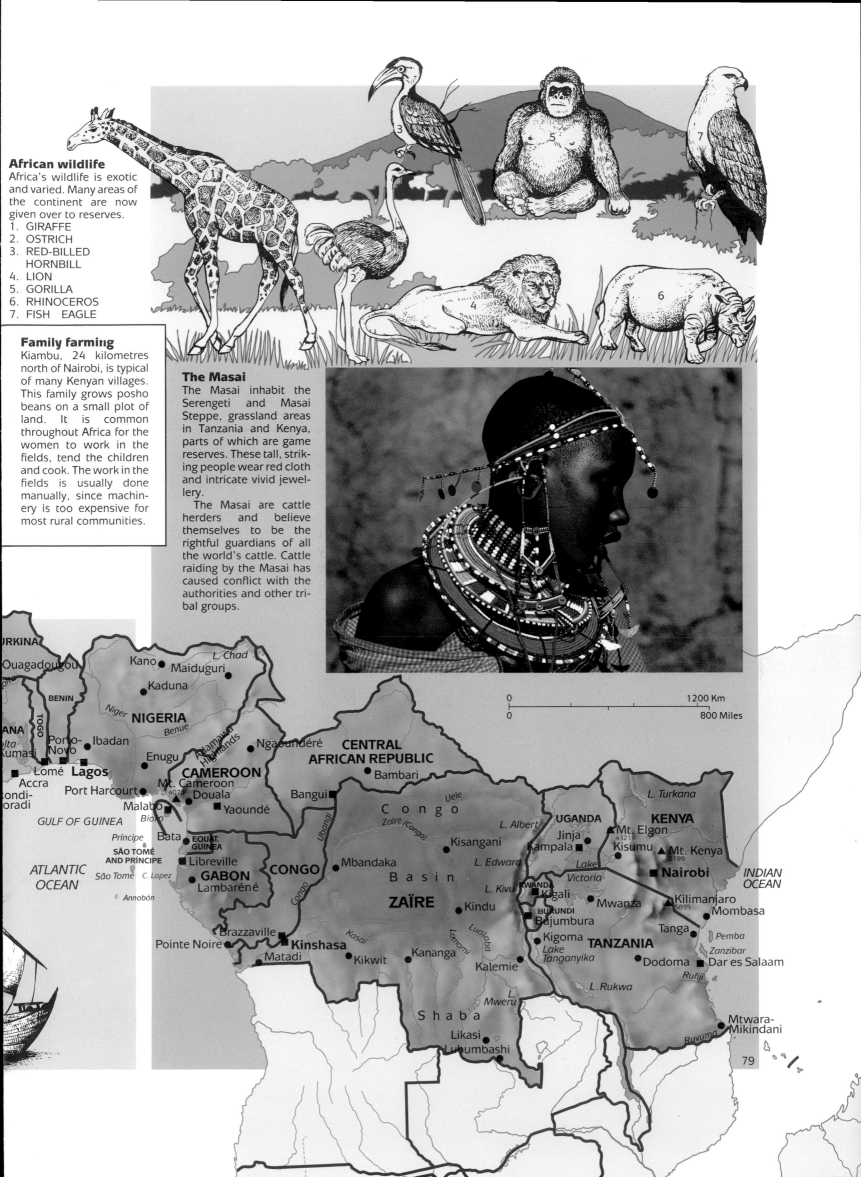

African wildlife

Africa's wildlife is exotic and varied. Many areas of the continent are now given over to reserves.

1. GIRAFFE
2. OSTRICH
3. RED-BILLED HORNBILL
4. LION
5. GORILLA
6. RHINOCEROS
7. FISH EAGLE

Family farming

Kiambu, 24 kilometres north of Nairobi, is typical of many Kenyan villages. This family grows posho beans on a small plot of land. It is common throughout Africa for the women to work in the fields, tend the children and cook. The work in the fields is usually done manually, since machinery is too expensive for most rural communities.

The Masai

The Masai inhabit the Serengeti and Masai Steppe, grassland areas in Tanzania and Kenya, parts of which are game reserves. These tall, striking people wear red cloth and intricate vivid jewellery.

The Masai are cattle herders and believe themselves to be the rightful guardians of all the world's cattle. Cattle raiding by the Masai has caused conflict with the authorities and other tribal groups.

SOUTHERN AFRICA

The countries to the south of Angola, Zambia and Mozambique are all part of southern Africa. The landscape across this region varies from the hot, dry areas of the Namib Desert in Namibia and the Kalahari in Botswana, to the vast, open grasslands of the *veldt* in South Africa and the lush low-lying plains which cover most of Mozambique.

The economies of most of the southern African countries rely heavily on the wealth resulting from the export of minerals. This region contains one of the greatest concentrations of valuable mineral resources in the world. Botswana, South Africa and Zimbabwe have some of the world's richest diamond deposits as well as huge coal reserves.

South Africa is the richest and most developed of all the countries in this region but is politically unstable as it operates a system called 'apartheid' which discriminates between people of different races. Although this situation is now improving, many countries still refuse to trade with South Africa as a result.

Kokerboom Forest, Namibia
The Kokerboom tree is also known as the 'quiver tree', because the Bushmen used to make pincushion-type quivers for their arrows from its fibrous core. The trees thrive in the arid land of central Namibia because they store water and can resist drought for years.

Agriculture in Zambia
In order to provide food for Africa's ever-growing population, agriculture must be developed. One option is to improve farming techniques in the villages. Alternatively, large-scale projects can be adopted, such as the Mpongwe scheme in Zambia which produces soya beans.

Bushmen of the Kalahari
Bushmen women from the Kalahari region making jewellery from tiny fragments of ostrich shells.

Mineral resources in southern Africa

Rich mineral deposits exist throughout southern and south-western Africa. This diamond mine in Angolia is one of many in this region.

Zimbabwe and South Africa both mine gold. However the industry is much larger in South Africa where Johannesburg is the world's gold mining centre.

Mining for other elements is widespread, particularly in South Africa where platinum, uranium and coal are produced. However the recycling of metals such as aluminium and steel is now becoming common throughout the world. This saves energy and resources but is reducing the demand for some minerals and so also diminishing their value.

The wildlife of southern Africa

A huge variety of wildlife is found in southern Africa. In the grasslands of South Africa the many species of antelope, such as the eland and oryx, are hunted by lions and cheetah. Huge herds of wildebeest roam the plains, and groups of giraffe and elephants wander around the waterholes. Leopards live in mountainous regions including those in Malawi and Zimbabwe. In the Okavango swamp in Botswana, hippo and crocodiles are abundant.

Madagascar is separated from mainland Africa by a considerable distance which has caused the animals there to evolve independently. A great number of species are unique to the island, including many varieties of the monkey-like lemur.

1. HYENA
2. CHIMPANZEE
3. AARDVARK
4. LEMUR

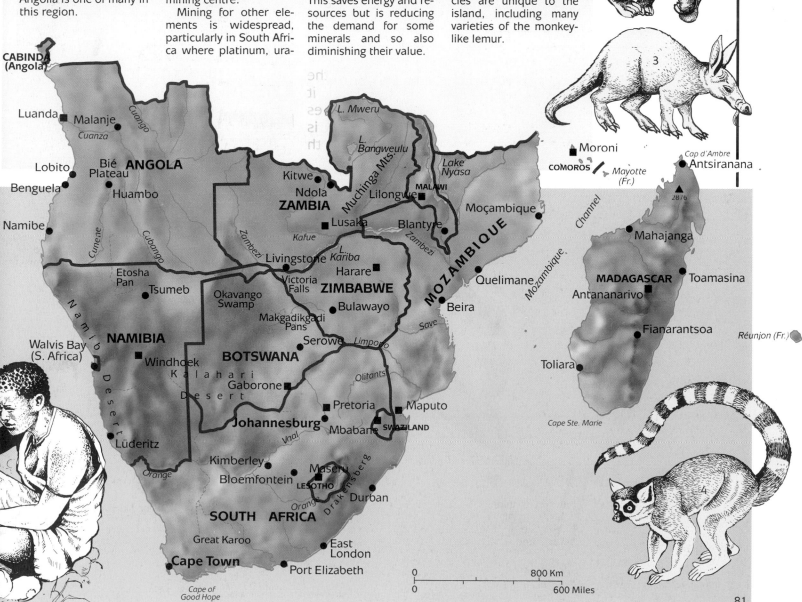

OCEANIA

Oceania is the name given to the region which includes Australia, New Zealand and the islands which are scattered across the Pacific Ocean. These islands are grouped into three areas: Melanesia, Micronesia and Polynesia. No-one knows exactly how many Pacific islands there are, but it is estimated that the total lies between twenty and thirty thousand. Some are coral islands while others, such as Hawaii, are volcanoes rising above the sea.

One of Australia's most famous attractions lies not on the land but in the sea. It is the beautiful Great Barrier Reef, which stretches for 2000 kilometres off the north-east coast. Farther south New Zealand's two main islands have a cooler, wetter climate than Australia, and a landscape which varies from mountainous Alps to rolling, green plains.

Oceania
Highest point Mount Cook (New Zealand) 3764m. (12,349ft.) above sea level
Lowest point Lake Eyre (Australia) 16m. (52ft.) below sea level
Longest river Murray-Darling (Australia) 3750km. (2330mi.)
Largest lake Lake Eyre (Australia) 9500 sq.km. (3700 sq.mi.)

AUSTRALIA
Area 7,682,300 sq. km. (2,966,151 sq. miles)
Population 16,468,600
Capital Canberra (pop. 257,850)
Currency Australian Dollar
Official language(s) English
Chief products Sheep, beef cattle, cereal, fruit, wine, wool, minerals, salt, coal, bauxite, wheat
Exports Wool, lamb, beef, cereals, dairy products, machinery, minerals, tobacco
Imports Alcoholic drinks, coal, oil, food, machinery
AUSTRALIAN STATES AND TERRITORIES
New South Wales
Area 801,600 sq. km. (309,500 sq. miles)
Population 5,612,244
Capital Sydney (pop. 3,472,700)
Victoria
Area 227,600 sq. km. (87,800 sq. miles)
Population 4,208,946

Capital Melbourne (pop. 2,931,900)
Queensland
Area 1,727,200 sq. km. (666,875 sq. miles)
Population 2,676,765
Capital Brisbane (pop. 1,196,000)
South Australia
Area 984,000 sq. km. (380,000 sq. miles)
Population 1,394,154
Capital Adelaide (pop. 1,003,800)
Western Australia
Area 2,525,500 sq. km. (975,000 sq. miles)
Population 1,500,507
Capital Perth (pop. 1,050,400)
Tasmania
Area 67,800 sq. km. (26,180 sq. miles)
Population 447,941
Capital Hobart (pop. 179,000)
Northern Territory
Area 1,346,200 sq. km. (520,000 sq. miles)
Population 156,674
Capital Darwin (pop. 74,800)
Australian Capital Territory
Area 2400 sq. km. (927 sq. miles)
Population 266,088
Capital Canberra

NEW ZEALAND
Area 267,844 sq. km. (103,415 sq. miles)
Population 3,349,200
Capital Wellington (pop. 324,400)
Largest cities Auckland (829,200) Christchurch (299,400) Dunedin (106,600) Hamilton (102,600)
Currency New Zealand Dollar
Official language(s) English (Maori is also spoken)
Chief products Sheep, wool, lamb, beef and dairy cattle, hardwood timber, minerals (especially coal, iron, sand), wheat, poultry, natural gas
Exports Iron ore, wheat, wool, live sheep and lambs, oil, petroleum products, beef, butter, kiwi fruit
Imports Machinery, electrical equipment, vehicles, iron and steel, textiles

PAPUA NEW GUINEA
Area 462,840 sq. km. (178,655 sq. miles)
Population 3,479,400
Capital Port Moresby
Official language(s) English (Pidgin English and Hiri Motu are also spoken)
Chief products Copper, silver, gold, minerals, oil and gas, paint, plywood, cocoa, copra, tea, coffee

FIJI
Official name Matanitu Ko Fiti
Area 18,330 sq. km. (7075 sq. miles)
Population 715,375
Capital Suva
Official language(s) English and Fijian
Chief products Sugar cane and molasses, coconuts, ginger, copra, fruit, fish, vegetables, rice, timber

PALAU

AUSTRALIA

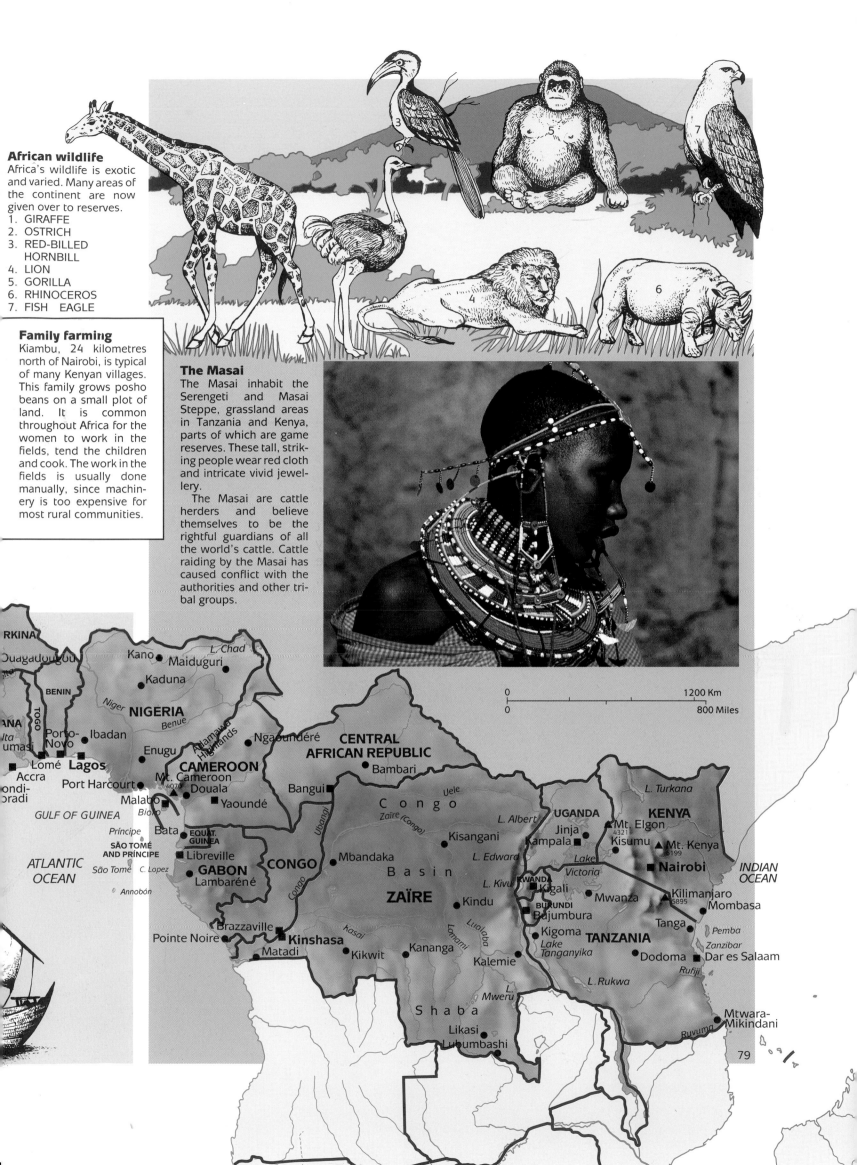

African wildlife

Africa's wildlife is exotic and varied. Many areas of the continent are now given over to reserves.

1. GIRAFFE
2. OSTRICH
3. RED-BILLED HORNBILL
4. LION
5. GORILLA
6. RHINOCEROS
7. FISH EAGLE

Family farming

Kiambu, 24 kilometres north of Nairobi, is typical of many Kenyan villages. This family grows posho beans on a small plot of land. It is common throughout Africa for the women to work in the fields, tend the children and cook. The work in the fields is usually done manually, since machinery is too expensive for most rural communities.

The Masai

The Masai inhabit the Serengeti and Masai Steppe, grassland areas in Tanzania and Kenya, parts of which are game reserves. These tall, striking people wear red cloth and intricate vivid jewellery.

The Masai are cattle herders and believe themselves to be the rightful guardians of all the world's cattle. Cattle raiding by the Masai has caused conflict with the authorities and other tribal groups.

SOUTHERN AFRICA

The countries to the south of Angola, Zambia and Mozambique are all part of southern Africa. The landscape across this region varies from the hot, dry areas of the Namib Desert in Namibia and the Kalahari in Botswana, to the vast, open grasslands of the *veldt* in South Africa and the lush low-lying plains which cover most of Mozambique.

The economies of most of the southern African countries rely heavily on the wealth resulting from the export of minerals. This region contains one of the greatest concentrations of valuable mineral resources in the world. Botswana, South Africa and Zimbabwe have some of the world's richest diamond deposits as well as huge coal reserves.

South Africa is the richest and most developed of all the countries in this region but is politically unstable as it operates a system called 'apartheid' which discriminates between people of different races. Although this situation is now improving, many countries still refuse to trade with South Africa as a result.

Kokerboom Forest, Namibia
The Kokerboom tree is also known as the 'quiver tree', because the Bushmen used to make pincushion-type quivers for their arrows from its fibrous core. The trees thrive in the arid land of central Namibia because they store water and can resist drought for years.

Agriculture in Zambia
In order to provide food for Africa's ever-growing population, agriculture must be developed. One option is to improve farming techniques in the villages. Alternatively, large-scale projects can be adopted, such as the Mpongwe scheme in Zambia which produces soya beans.

Bushmen of the Kalahari
Bushmen women from the Kalahari region making jewellery from tiny fragments of ostrich shells.

The wildlife of southern Africa

A huge variety of wildlife is found in southern Africa. In the grasslands of South Africa the many species of antelope, such as the eland and oryx, are hunted by lions and cheetah. Huge herds of wildebeest roam the plains, and groups of giraffe and elephants wander around the waterholes. Leopards live in mountainous regions including those in Malawi and Zimbabwe. In the Okavango swamp in Botswana, hippo and crocodiles are abundant.

Madagascar is separated from mainland Africa by a considerable distance which has caused the animals there to evolve independently. A great number of species are unique to the island, including many varieties of the monkey-like lemur.

1. HYENA
2. CHIMPANZEE
3. AARDVARK
4. LEMUR

Mineral resources in southern Africa

Rich mineral deposits exist throughout southern and south-western Africa. This diamond mine in Angola is one of many in this region.

Zimbabwe and South Africa both mine gold. However the industry is much larger in South Africa where Johannesburg is the world's gold mining centre.

Mining for other elements is widespread, particularly in South Africa where platinum, uranium and coal are produced. However the recycling of metals such as aluminium and steel is now becoming common throughout the world. This saves energy and resources but is reducing the demand for some minerals and so also diminishing their value.

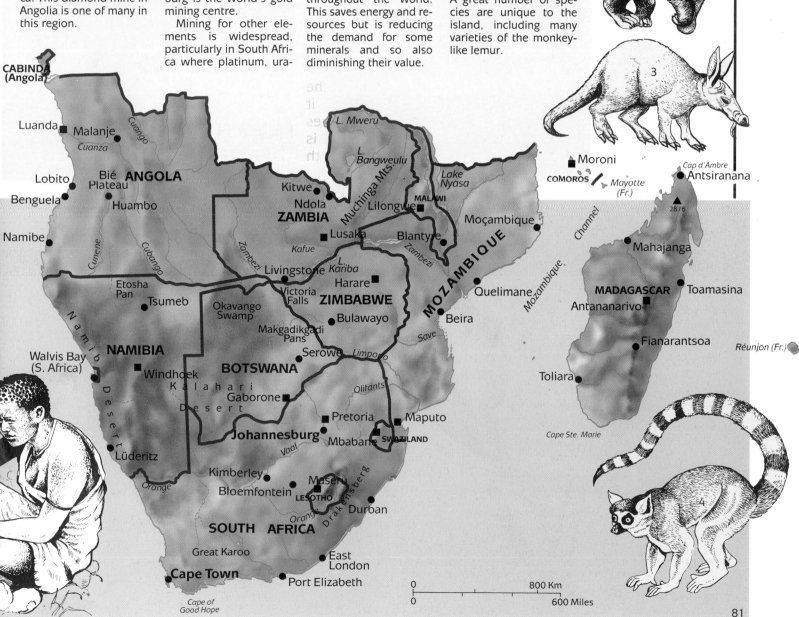

CABINDA (Angola)

Luanda
Malanje
Cuanza
Cuanza
Cuango

Lobito
Bié Plateau
ANGOLA

Benguela
Huambo

Namibe

Cunene
Cubango

Etosha Pan
Tsumeb

Namib Desert

Walvis Bay (S. Africa)
NAMIBIA

Lüderitz
Orange

Windhoek
Kalahari Desert

Okavango Swamp
Makgadikgadi Pans
Serowe

BOTSWANA
Gaborone

L. Mweru
L. Bangweulu

Kitwe
Ndola
ZAMBIA
Lusaka
Kafue

Muchinga Mts.
Lilongwe
MALAWI
Lake Nyasa

Blantyre
Zambezi

Moçambique

MOZAMBIQUE

Quelimane

Beira

Save

Zambezi
Livingstone
L. Kariba
Victoria Falls
Harare
ZIMBABWE
Bulawayo
Limpopo
Olifants

Pretoria
Maputo
Mbabane
SWAZILAND
Johannesburg
Vaal

Kimberley
Maseru
Bloemfontein
LESOTHO
Orange

Durban
Drakensberg

SOUTH AFRICA

Great Karoo
Cape Town
Port Elizabeth
Cape of Good Hope

East London

Moroni
COMOROS
Mayotte (Fr.)

Cap d'Ambre
Antsiranana

2876

Mahajanga

Mozambique Channel

MADAGASCAR
Toamasina
Antananarivo

Fianarantsoa

Réunion (Fr.)

Toliara

Cape Ste. Marie

0   800 Km
0   600 Miles

OCEANIA

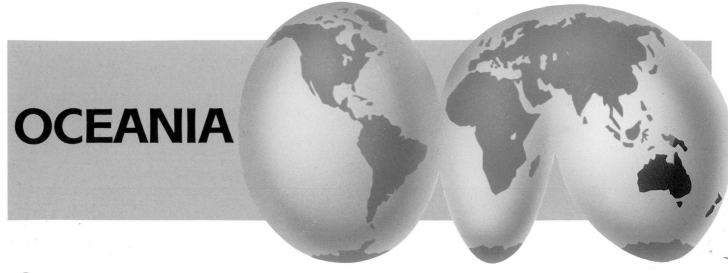

Oceania is the name given to the region which includes Australia, New Zealand and the islands which are scattered across the Pacific Ocean. These islands are grouped into three areas: Melanesia, Micronesia and Polynesia. No-one knows exactly how many Pacific islands there are, but it is estimated that the total lies between twenty and thirty thousand. Some are coral islands while others, such as Hawaii, are volcanoes rising above the sea.

One of Australia's most famous attractions lies not on the land but in the sea. It is the beautiful Great Barrier Reef, which stretches for 2000 kilometres off the north-east coast. Farther south New Zealand's two main islands have a cooler, wetter climate than Australia, and a landscape which varies from mountainous Alps to rolling, green plains.

Oceania
Highest point Mount Cook (New Zealand) 3764m. (12,349ft.) above sea level
Lowest point Lake Eyre (Australia) 16m. (52ft.) below sea level
Longest river Murray-Darling (Australia) 3750km. (2330mi.)
Largest lake Lake Eyre (Australia) 9500 sq.km. (3700 sq.mi.)

AUSTRALIA
Area 7,682,300 sq. km. (2,966,151 sq. miles)
Population 16,468,600
Capital Canberra (pop. 257,850)
Currency Australian Dollar
Official language(s) English
Chief products Sheep, beef cattle, cereal, fruit, wine, wool, minerals, salt, coal, bauxite, wheat
Exports Wool, lamb, beef, cereals, dairy products, machinery, minerals, tobacco
Imports Alcoholic drinks, coal, oil, food, machinery
AUSTRALIAN STATES AND TERRITORIES
New South Wales
Area 801,600 sq. km. (309,500 sq. miles)
Population 5,612,244
Capital Sydney (pop. 3,472,700)
Victoria
Area 227,600 sq. km. (87,800 sq. miles)
Population 4,208,946

Capital Melbourne (pop. 2,931,900)
Queensland
Area 1,727,200 sq. km. (666,875 sq. miles)
Population 2,676,765
Capital Brisbane (pop. 1,196,000)
South Australia
Area 984,000 sq. km. (380,000 sq. miles)
Population 1,394,154
Capital Adelaide (pop. 1,003,800)
Western Australia
Area 2,525,500 sq. km. (975,000 sq. miles)
Population 1,500,507
Capital Perth (pop. 1,050,400)
Tasmania
Area 67,800 sq. km. (26,180 sq. miles)
Population 447,941
Capital Hobart (pop. 179,000)
Northern Territory
Area 1,346,200 sq. km. (520,000 sq. miles)
Population 156,674
Capital Darwin (pop. 74,800)
Australian Capital Territory
Area 2400 sq. km. (927 sq. miles)
Population 266,088
Capital Canberra

NEW ZEALAND
Area 267,844 sq. km. (103,415 sq. miles)
Population 3,349,200
Capital Wellington (pop. 324,400)
Largest cities Auckland (829,200)
Christchurch (299,400)
Dunedin (106,600)
Hamilton (102,600)
Currency New Zealand Dollar
Official language(s) English (Maori is also spoken)
Chief products Sheep, wool, lamb, beef and dairy cattle, hardwood timber, minerals (especially coal, iron, sand), wheat, poultry, natural gas
Exports Iron ore, wheat, wool, live sheep and lambs, oil, petroleum products, beef, butter, kiwi fruit
Imports Machinery, electrical equipment, vehicles, iron and steel, textiles

PAPUA NEW GUINEA
Area 462,840 sq. km. (178,655 sq. miles)
Population 3,479,400
Capital Port Moresby
Official language(s) English (Pidgin English and Hiri Motu are also spoken)
Chief products Copper, silver, gold, minerals, oil and gas, paint, plywood, cocoa, copra, tea, coffee

FIJI
Official name Matanitu Ko Fiti
Area 18,330 sq. km. (7075 sq. miles)
Population 715,375
Capital Suva
Official language(s) English and Fijian
Chief products Sugar cane and molasses, coconuts, ginger, copra, fruit, fish, vegetables, rice, timber

NAME	AREA SQ. KM. (SQ. MILES)	POPULATION	CAPITAL
Cook Islands (NZ)	293 (113)	17,185	Avarua
French Polynesia	3940 (1520)	188,814	Papeete
Guam (USA)	549 (212)	129,254	Agaña
Kiribati	684 (284)	66,000	Bairiki
Marshall Islands (USA)	180 (70)	34,923	Dalap-Uligara-Darrit
The Federated States of Micronesia (USA)	330 (127)	86,094	–
Nauru	21.3 (8.2)	8042	Yaren
New Caledonia (Fr)	19,058 (7358)	153,000	Noumea
Niue (NZ)	259 (100)	2190	Alofi
Norfolk Is. (Aus)	34.5 (13.3)	1977	Kingston
Palau (USA)	367 (142)	14,106	Koror
Northern Marianas (US)	476 (184)	22,000	Saipan
Pitcairn Islands (UK)	45 (17.25)	57	–
Samoa (USA)	196 (76)	34,500	Pago Pago
Solomon Islands	29,790 (11,500)	285,796	Honiara
Tonga	699 (270)	111,000	Nuku'alofa
Tuvalu	24.6 (9.5)	8229	Funafuti
Vanuatu	14,763 (5700)	140,154	Port Vila
Wallis and Futuna Is. (Fr)	274 (106)	13,100	Mata-Utu
Western Samoa	2840 (1095)	163,000	Apia

KIRIBATI

TONGA

NAURU

TUVALU

PALAU

VANUATU

SOLOMON IS.

WESTERN SAMOA

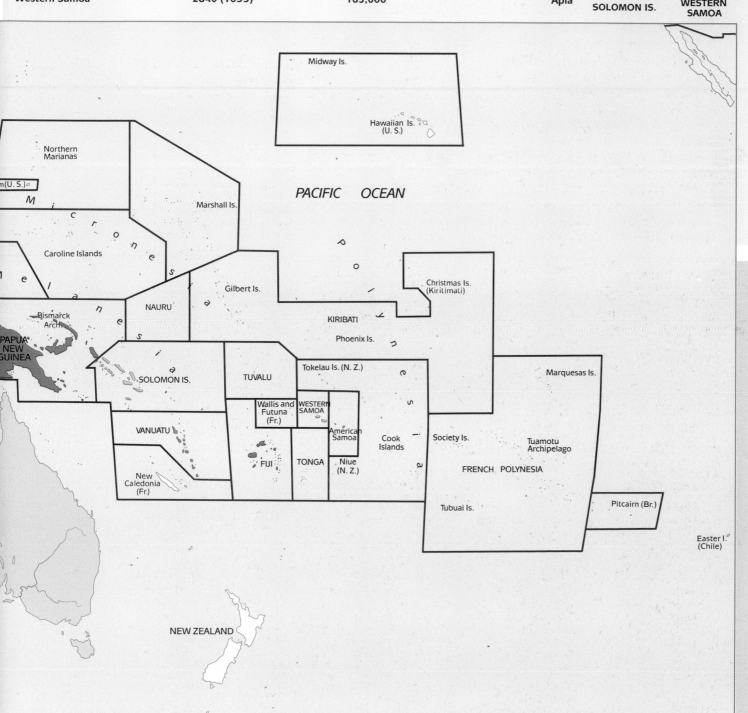

AUSTRALIA

Australia is made up of five mainland states and two territories, and the island state of Tasmania. The arid interior of the continent, known as the outback, is virtually uninhabited, but in areas where water can be found there are huge cattle stations and sheep farms – Australia is the world's largest producer of wool.

Eighty per cent of the Australian population lives in cities, almost all of which are located in the fertile area in the south-east between Adelaide and Brisbane, and around Perth in Western Australia. Fewer than 50,000 Aborigines, the native people of Australia, survive. Some cling to their traditional ways of life, but most have moved to the cities, or live on special reserves set aside for them by the government.

Australia is one of the world's largest mineral producers – bauxite (aluminium ore), copper, iron ore and coal are all found in abundance in north and west Australia.

A sheep auction
Australia is the world's chief wool-producing country. Here, Merino sheep are being sold at an auction. The Merino is specially bred for its fine quality wool.

Ayers Rock
Ayers Rock is Australia's most famous landmark. It is three kilometres long and almost nine kilometres round. It lies in the middle of the vast flat desert lands of central Australia. The Rock is sacred to the Aborigines – inside it are caves with paintings and carvings on the walls which depict stories of their ancestors. It is known to the Aborigines as Uluru.

Surfing off Bondi beach
A surf lifesaver on one of the golden beaches near Sydney in south-eastern Australia. Beaches such as Bondi and Tamarama are only eight kilometres from the city centre.

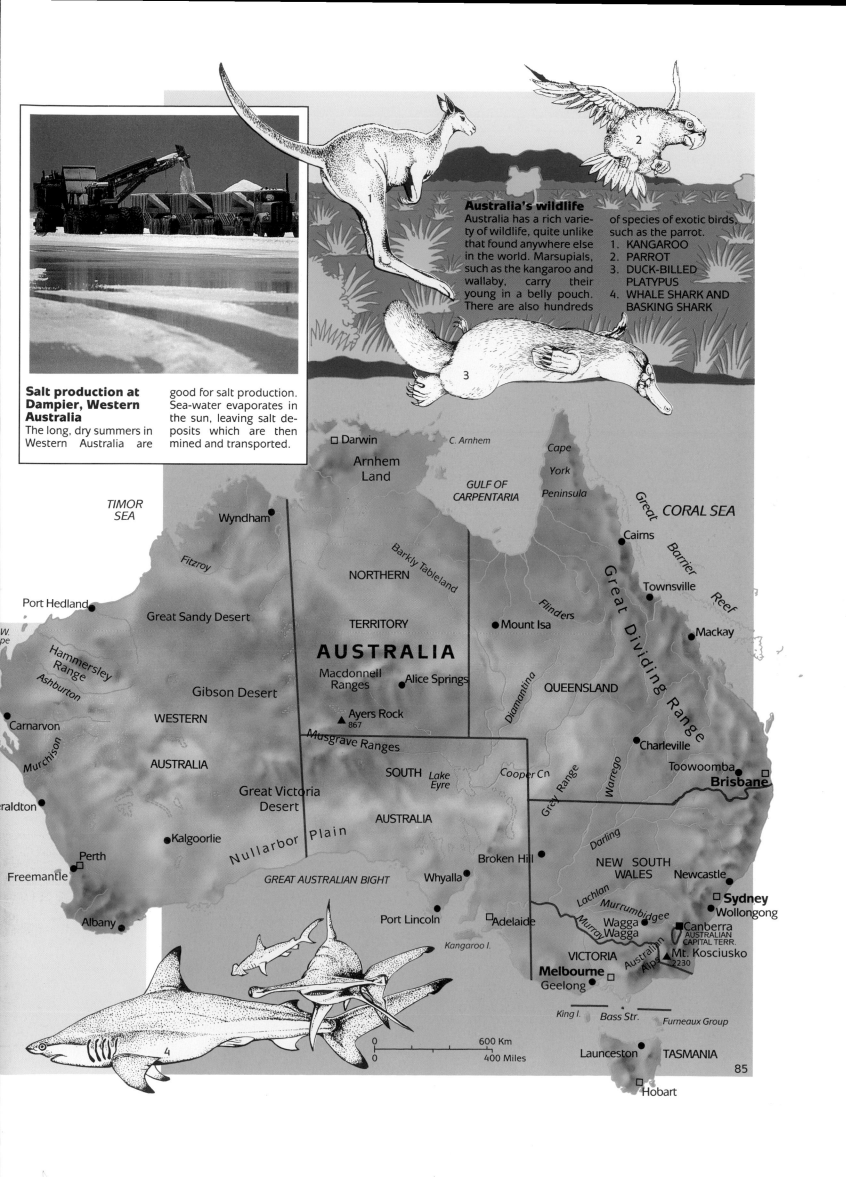

Salt production at Dampier, Western Australia

The long, dry summers in Western Australia are good for salt production. Sea-water evaporates in the sun, leaving salt deposits which are then mined and transported.

Australia's wildlife

Australia has a rich variety of wildlife, quite unlike that found anywhere else in the world. Marsupials, such as the kangaroo and wallaby, carry their young in a belly pouch. There are also hundreds of species of exotic birds, such as the parrot.

1. KANGAROO
2. PARROT
3. DUCK-BILLED PLATYPUS
4. WHALE SHARK AND BASKING SHARK

TIMOR SEA

Darwin

C. Arnhem

Arnhem Land

GULF OF CARPENTARIA

Cape York Peninsula

Great CORAL SEA

Wyndham

Fitzroy

Barkly Tableland

NORTHERN

Cairns

Barrier

Great Dividing Range

Port Hedland

Great Sandy Desert

TERRITORY

Flinders

Townsville

Mount Isa

Mackay

Hammersley Range

Ashburton

AUSTRALIA

Macdonnell Ranges

Alice Springs

QUEENSLAND

Carnarvon

Gibson Desert

WESTERN

Ayers Rock
867

Diamantina

Charleville

AUSTRALIA

Musgrave Ranges

eraldton

Great Victoria Desert

SOUTH

Lake Eyre

Cooper Cn

Grey Range

Warrego

Toowoomba

Brisbane

AUSTRALIA

Darling

Kalgoorlie

Nullarbor Plain

Perth

Broken Hill

NEW SOUTH WALES

Newcastle

Freemantle

GREAT AUSTRALIAN BIGHT

Whyalla

Lachlan

Murrumbidgee

Sydney

Wollongong

Albany

Port Lincoln

Adelaide

Murray

Wagga Wagga

Canberra
AUSTRALIAN CAPITAL TERR.

Kangaroo I.

VICTORIA

Australian Alps

Mt. Kosciusko
2230

Melbourne

Geelong

King I.

Bass Str.

Furneaux Group

0   600 Km

0   400 Miles

Launceston

TASMANIA

85

Hobart

NEW ZEALAND

New Zealand consists of two large islands and a number of smaller ones. Parts of North Island are volcanically active, with bubbling mud pools and geysers which shoot boiling water up to 100 metres in the air. As well as being a tourist attraction, the geysers produce steam which is used to generate electricity. The lower mountain slopes and green plains on South Island provide ideal grazing land for sheep.

Most of the population of New Zealand lives on North Island and is descended from the Europeans who settled in the nineteenth and twentieth centuries. The native inhabitants of the country, the Maoris, are now in the minority.

New Zealand's economy is based around agriculture – especially the export of dairy produce, meat, and specialized food such as kiwifruit. Recently, reserves of natural gas off the west coast have been discovered, and wood-pulp and iron export industries have been established.

The Maoris
Wood carving is a traditional craft of the Maoris, the original inhabitants who came by canoe from other Pacific islands to New Zealand in about AD 800. The wood carvings, which show aspects of traditional Maori life, are mostly produced today for sale to tourists. Another traditional craft is the fashioning of jewel-lery, made from semi-precious stones and gems found on the islands.

Wellington
This is the port at Wellington, the small administrative capital of New Zealand, which is situated at the southern tip of North Island. It is characterized by steep hills, earthquakes and year-round gusting winds – its nickname is the 'windy city'. From the port, the Picton Ferry provides a link between North and South Islands. About sixty per cent of all exports, primarily dairy produce and lamb, is shipped in huge refrigerated containers from here to Europe, the USA and Japan. The remainder is transported from Auckland farther north.

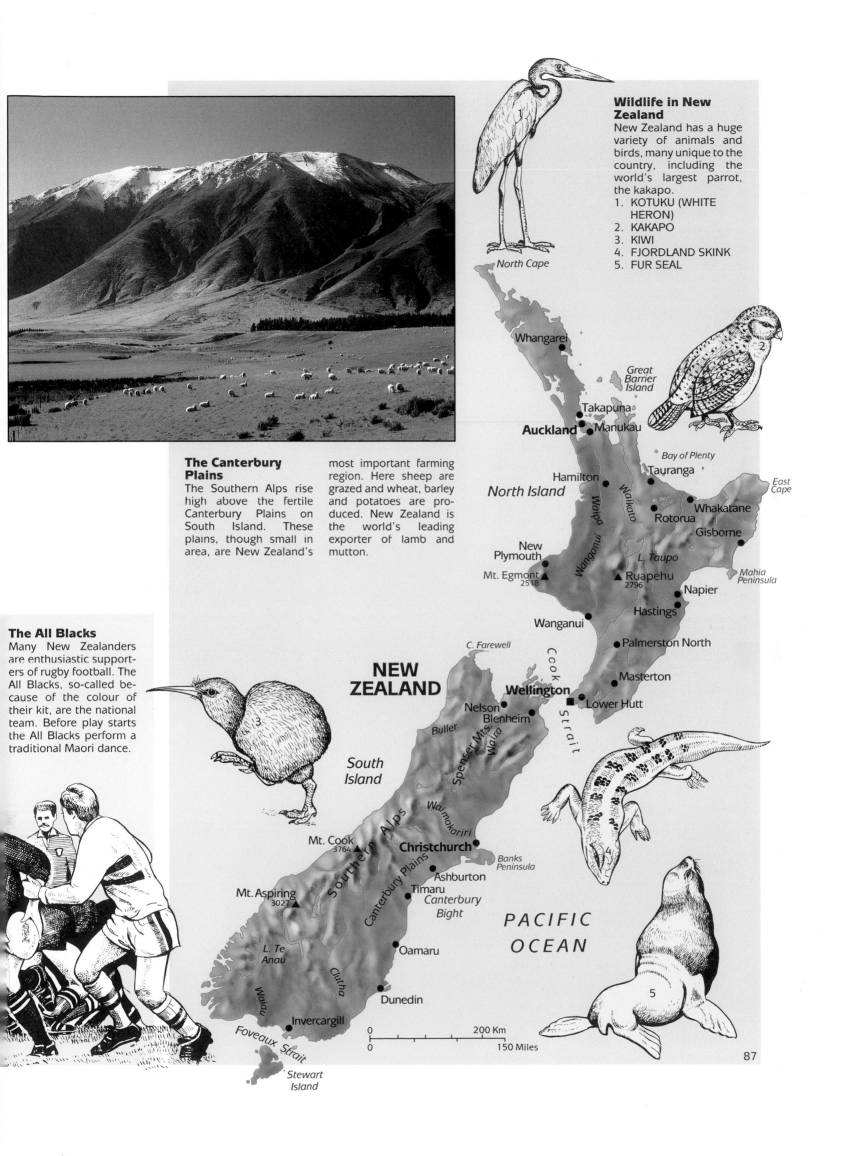

Wildlife in New Zealand

New Zealand has a huge variety of animals and birds, many unique to the country, including the world's largest parrot, the kakapo.

1. KOTUKU (WHITE HERON)
2. KAKAPO
3. KIWI
4. FJORDLAND SKINK
5. FUR SEAL

The Canterbury Plains

The Southern Alps rise high above the fertile Canterbury Plains on South Island. These plains, though small in area, are New Zealand's most important farming region. Here sheep are grazed and wheat, barley and potatoes are produced. New Zealand is the world's leading exporter of lamb and mutton.

The All Blacks

Many New Zealanders are enthusiastic supporters of rugby football. The All Blacks, so-called because of the colour of their kit, are the national team. Before play starts the All Blacks perform a traditional Maori dance.

North Cape

Whangarei

Great Barrier Island

Takapuna
Auckland Manukau

Bay of Plenty

Hamilton
North Island
Tauranga

East Cape

Waipa

Waikato

Rotorua

Whakatane

Gisborne

New Plymouth

Wanganui

L. Taupo

Mt. Egmont ▲ 2518

▲ Ruapehu 2796

Mahia Peninsula

Napier

Wanganui

Hastings

C. Farewell

Palmerston North

NEW ZEALAND

Cook Strait

Masterton

Wellington ■ Lower Hutt

Nelson
Blenheim

Buller

Spenser Mts.

Waira

South Island

Waimakariri

Southern Alps

Mt. Cook ▲ 3764

Christchurch

Banks Peninsula

Canterbury Plains

Ashburton

Mt. Aspiring ▲ 3027

Timaru
Canterbury Bight

Clutha

L. Te Anau

Oamaru

PACIFIC OCEAN

Waiau

Dunedin

Invercargill

Foveaux Strait

| 0 | | 200 Km |
| 0 | 150 Miles | |

Stewart Island

87

PACIFIC ISLANDS

The islands scattered across the Pacific Ocean, south-east of Asia, are grouped into three regions: Melanesia, which includes the largest island in the Pacific region, Papua New Guinea, Micronesia, and Polynesia which extends north to Hawaii and east to include Easter Island.

The original settlers of the islands are thought to have come by sea from south-east Asia. Today the Pacific islanders are still expert seafarers, and many of the smaller islands' economies rely on fishing. Much of the agriculture on the islands is subsistence farming. In the tropical climate yams, breadfruit, sweet potatoes and fruits are grown and sold in local markets. Larger islands such as Papua New Guinea also grow coffee, copra and cocoa for export. Valuable minerals reserves on some islands are an important source of income: New Caledonia is the third largest producer of nickel in the world, Christmas Island has large phosphate supplies and copper is mined on Papua New Guinea.

FIJI

```
0          150 Km
0          100 Miles
```

Vanua Levu   Udu Pt.
                  Ringgold Is.
Lambasa   Rambi

Yasawa Group
Bligh Water   Taveuni
                          Nanuku Passage
Viti Levu
                   Koro   Vanua Mbalavu
                          Mango
Lautoka   ● Tavua
          ▲ Tomanlivi   KORO SEA   Thithia
            1322   Ovalau
                   Ngau   Lakemba Passage
                                  Lakemba
Singatoka   ■ Suva

Vatulele   Moala
        Kandavu Passage
                      Kambara
                 Totoya
        Kandavu   Matuku

Lau (Eastern) Group

Modern ways
Until recently, many of the Pacific islands were undeveloped and the people lived as they had for thousands of years. Development of the islands by outsiders, has changed the traditional way of life dramatically. Younger people in particular have adopted many 'western' ways.

South Sea paradise
This idyllic view near Bora Bora in the French Polynesian islands is typical of much of the scenery in the South Seas. The beauty of the surroundings and the tropical climate are attracting more and more visitors every year. Some islands, such as Fiji, are developing luxury resorts to encourage the extra revenue that tourism brings.

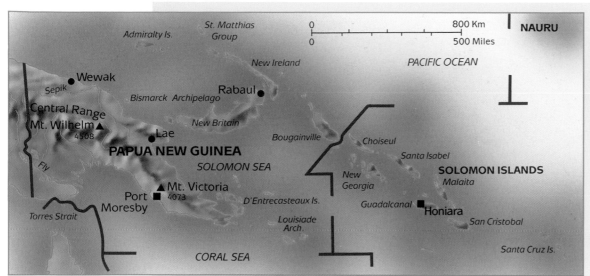

St. Matthias Group

Admiralty Is.

NAURU

PACIFIC OCEAN

New Ireland

Wewak

Sepik

Rabaul

Bismarck Archipelago

Central Range

New Britain

Mt. Wilhelm▲
4508

Lae

Bougainville

Choiseul

PAPUA NEW GUINEA

SOLOMON SEA

Santa Isabel

Fly

New
Georgia

SOLOMON ISLANDS

Malaita

Mt. Victoria
4073

D'Entrecasteaux Is.

Port
Moresby

Guadalcanal

Honiara

San Cristobal

Torres Strait

Louisiade
Arch.

CORAL SEA

Santa Cruz Is.

0 — 800 Km
0 — 500 Miles

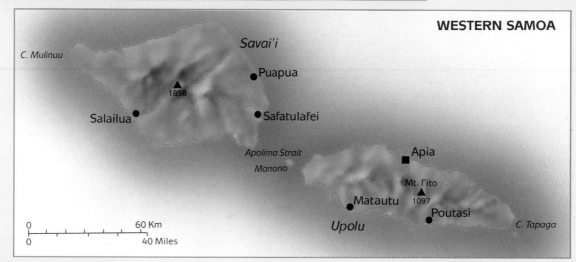

WESTERN SAMOA

C. Mulinuu

Savai'i

Puapua

1858

Salailua

Safatulafei

Apolima Strait

Apia

Manono

Mt. Fito
1097

Matautu

Poutasi

Upolu

C. Tapaga

0 — 60 Km
0 — 40 Miles

Coconut wealth

Copra, the dry white flesh of the coconut, being stored at Port Moresby Wharf in Papua New Guinea, ready for export. Copra brings wealth to many Pacific islands. It is prepared by removing the fibrous husk of the coconut, splitting the nut and laying out strips of the white 'meat' to dry in the sun. The meat is then crushed to extract the oil.

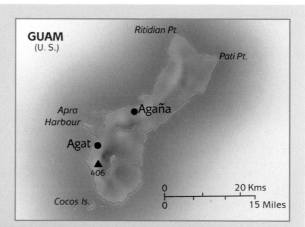

GUAM
(U. S.)

Ritidian Pt.

Pati Pt.

Apra
Harbour

Agaña

Agat

406

Cocos Is.

0 — 20 Kms
0 — 15 Miles

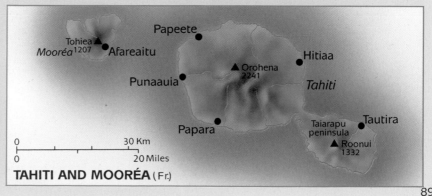

Papeete

Tohiea▲
Mooréa 1207

Afareaitu

Hitiaa

▲ Orohena
2241

Punaauia

Tahiti

Papara

Taiarapu
peninsula

Tautira

▲ Roonui
1332

0 — 30 Km
0 — 20 Miles

TAHITI AND MOORÉA (Fr.)

ARCTIC AND ANTARCTIC

The Arctic and Antarctica are remote, ice-bound regions around the two Poles. At the North Pole a layer of ice about six metres deep floats within the Arctic Ocean. At the South Pole the ice cap is on average 2300 metres thick over the buried land mass of Antarctica.

Both regions are extremely cold. However, during summer in the northern hemisphere the snow and ice melt in parts of the Arctic, and moss, lichen and flowers appear. About two million people live within the Arctic Circle, including the Inuit of Alaska and Greenland. No-one lives permanently in Antarctica, although scientists have set up camps there to study the environment.

The Arctic is rich in mineral resources including fossil fuels, diamonds and gold. These are being exploited by the surrounding countries. Antarctica is rich in food resources from the sea, but in accordance with international agreement, it has remained untouched so far.

Research in Antarctica

The first explorers reached Antarctica in the early part of this century. Today, researchers from many countries have set up stations in the inhospitable conditions, and even grow their own vegetables in heated greenhouses. Scientific research suggests that huge reserves of natural resources such as oil and

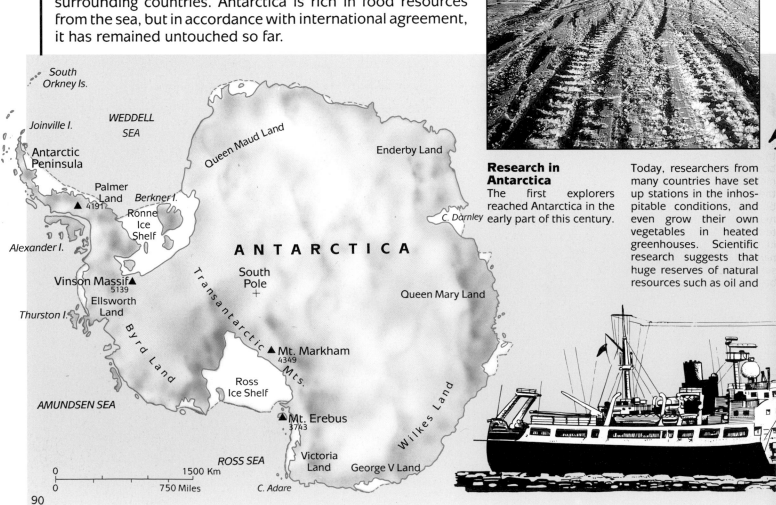

South Orkney Is.

WEDDELL SEA

Joinville I.

Antarctic Peninsula

Palmer Land · Berkner I.

▲ 4191

Ronne Ice Shelf

Alexander I.

Queen Maud Land

Enderby Land

C. Darnley

ANTARCTICA

South Pole +

Queen Mary Land

Vinson Massif ▲ 5139

Transantarctic

Ellsworth Land

Thurston I.

Byrd Land

▲ Mt. Markham 4349

Mts.

Ross Ice Shelf

Wilkes Land

AMUNDSEN SEA

▲ Mt. Erebus 3743

ROSS SEA

Victoria Land

George V Land

0   1500 Km

0   750 Miles

C. Adare

Animals in the cold

The Poles and the surrounding seas support a huge variety of wildlife, despite the extreme cold.

1. ARCTIC SKUA
2. POLAR BEAR
3. WALRUS
4. KILLER WHALE

gas exist in the region, though no oil has yet been found. Nineteen nations have laid claim to the potential wealth buried in Antarctica, and many more are interested. A treaty signed in 1961, in which the 19 nations agreed to conserve the region, is due to be renewed in 1991.

JOHN BISCOE

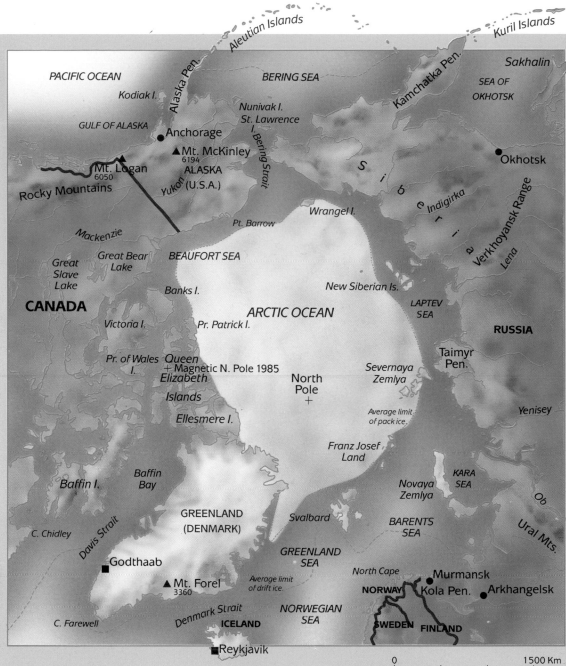

Dying traditions

The ancestors of these Inuit children lived in isolated communities in the Arctic, and survived by hunting and fishing. They caught caribou and reindeer, which provided them with meat, and skins for making clothes and tents. When they moved on to search for food, teams of dogs pulled the sledges.

Today the Arctic is no longer so isolated. Since the discovery of oil, mining communities have sprung up and with them schools, shops and hospitals. The traditional way of life has been destroyed and most of the Inuit now live in permanent homes in these mining communities.

91

GENERAL INDEX

Page numbers in *italics* refer to illustrations

92

MAP INDEX

Page numbers in **bold** refer to entries in the country information files.

Acknowledgements
The publishers would like to thank the following for the use of their pictures:

ZEFA Picture Library is indicated as **Z** throughout.
Tony Stone Worldwide is indicated as **TSW** throughout.

Page 1 TSW/S. & N. Geary; p3 TSW; p8 TSW/R. Passmore; p10 top Z/Eugen middle Z/Strachil; p11 TSW/N. Beer; p12 left Z/Edel top right Z/Damm bottom right Danish Dairy Board; p13 Z/Eugen; p14 left TSW/D. Higgs right TSW; p15 TSW; p16 left Robert Harding Picture Library/R. Curdy right TSW/C. Kempf; p17 top French Railways bottom Magnum/Zachmann; p18 left Z/Streichen right TSW/J. Yates; p19 Netherlands Board of Tourism; p20 left TSW/R. Everts right Z/Deuter; p21 Carla Arnold; p22 left Z/R. Nicolas right TSW/M. Mehlig; p23 TSW; p24 left Fiat right Hutchison Library; p25 TSW/M. Mehlig; p26 left TSW/S. Johnson right TSW/O. Benn; p27 Magnum/ M. Gruyaert; p28 left TSW/R. Everts right TSW/M. Caldwell; p29 top Z/Dr. H. Kramarz bottom Z; p30 left TSW/R. Everts right Z; p31 Magnum/E. Erwitt; p32 Frank Spooner Pictures/V. Shone; p33 Z; p34 top Linda Proud middle Z bottom Novosti; p35 Z; p36 TSW/J. Kopee; p38 top Z/Hunter bottom Z/K. Kummels; p39 TSW; p40 TSW/D. Schultz; p41 TSW; p42 top TSW/M. Segal middle Z/Stefnmans bottom Robert Harding Picture Library/ G. & P. Lorrigan; p43 TSW/M. Brooke; p44 Z; p45 left TSW/G. Prentice right Robert Harding Picture Library/G. & P. Lorrigan; p46 Hutchison Library/ P. Wolmuth; p47 top Robert Harding Picture Library bottom TSW/ W. Rudolph; p48 TSW/P. Gittoes; p49 Z; p50 TSW; p51 Z; p52 left Art Directors top right TSW/S. Cunningham bottom right Z/J. Heydecker; p54 left TSW/D. Levy right Hutchison Library; p55 top TSW/D. Levy bottom TSW/T. Zimmerman; p56 TSW; p58 top Z/ Maroon bottom Z; p60 left Mepha/Jill Brown right Sonia Halliday; p61 top Z bottom TSW; p62 left Planet Earth Pictures/H.C. Heap right Z; p63 TSW; p64 left Robert Harding Picture Library right Z/K. Schulz; p65 top TSW bottom Robert Harding Picture Library; p66 left TSW/A. Smith right Z/H. Raze; p67 Z/Sunak; p68 Robert Harding Picture Library; p69 TSW; p70 top TSW/A. le Garsmeur bottom TSW/Osmond; p71 Hutchison Picture Library; p72 left Photo Original right, TSW; p73 top Hutchison Picture Library bottom TSW; p74 Frank Spooner Pictures; p76 Z; p77 left Frank Spooner Pictures/M. Deville right Hutchison Picture Library; p78 left Hutchison Picture Library right Z/E. Earp; p79 TSW; p80 left TSW/I. Murphy right Robert Harding Picture Library/C. Jopp; p81 Hutchison Picture Library; p84 left TSW/S.&N. Geary right TSW; p85 TSW; p86 TSW/R. Smith; p87 TSW; p88 Z/ E. Christian; p89 Robert Harding Picture Library; p90 Robert Harding Picture Library/G. Renner; p91 Robert Harding Picture Library/W. Herbert.

Picture research by Linda Proud